HIGHEST PRAISE FOR
HAROLD J. ROTHWAX AND

GUILTY

◆ ◆ ◆

"Brace yourself for the rush of anger as GUILTY throws open the dark curtain that has shielded the criminal justice system from public scrutiny."
**—Philip K. Howard,
author of *The Death of Common Sense***

◆

"Should be required reading for anyone who cares about law and order, how it has been undermined, and what can be done to fix it."
—*New York Daily News*

◆

"Intensely felt and well written."
—*Washington Post*

◆

"Judge Rothwax is demonstrating what many people know—that the justice system has become a board game."
—New York City Mayor Rudolph Giuliani

◆

"Courageous. . . . An unblinking look at our disintegrating legal system. In clear, direct language, with story after story, the judge catalogues what you already suspect . . . [and] makes a persuasive case that it is time to challenge what the system has become."
—Rush Limbaugh, Limbaugh Letter

◆

"Blunt, forceful. . . . A compelling case that something is very wrong in the judicial system."
—*New York Times*

more . . .

"Stimulating and provocative. . . . He presents, with his customary clarity and frankness, his opinions as to the problems which afflict the criminal justice system. . . . He also offers his solutions."
—*New York Law Journal*

◆

"A mad-as-hell manifesto. . . . Rothwax minces no words."
—*Booklist*

◆

"Bold . . . logical. . . . Rothwax's suggestion that jury verdicts of 10-2 be allowed will surely become part of the debate over our court system in these post–O.J. days."
—*Publishers Weekly*

◆

"Informative . . . keen observations . . . Rothwax brings a reporter's tenacity and a novelist's touch to his work."
—*The State* (SC)

◆

"A grim verdict on the system."
—*New York Post*

◆

"A very readable book filled with thought-provoking questions that are well illustrated with examples from real cases."
—*Patriot* (PA)

◆

"A splendid diagnostician of the failures of liberal criminal justice."
—*Weekly Standard* magazine

Guilty

The Collapse of
Criminal Justice

Judge
Harold J. Rothwax

WARNER BOOKS

A Time Warner Company

Warner Books Edition
Copyright © 1996 by Harold J. Rothwax
All rights reserved.

This Warner Books edition is published by arrangement with Random House, Inc., New York, NY

Warner Books, Inc., 1271 Avenue of the Americas, New York, NY 10020

Visit our Web site at
http://pathfinder.com/twep

A Time Warner Company

Ⓦ Printed in the United States of America

First Trade Printing: January 1997
10 9 8 7 6 5 4 3 2 1

Library of Congress Cataloging-in-Publication Data
Rothwax, Harold J.
        Guilty : the collapse of criminal justice / Harold J. Rothwax.
            p.   cm.
        Originally published: 1st ed. New York : Random House, c1996.
        ISBN 0-446-67304-8
        1. Criminal justice, Administration of—United States.
    2. Adversary system (Law)—United States. 3. Law reform—United States.
    I. Title.
    KF9223.R68   1997
    345.73′05—dc20
    [347.3055]   96-28845
                                                        CIP

Cover design by Andy Carpenter
Author photograph by James Hamilton

To Yona, Julia, and Louis

*and for my mother
in beloved memory*

———

The Court is forever adding new stories to the temples of constitutional law, and the temples have a way of collapsing when one story too many is added.

JUSTICE ROBERT H. JACKSON,
U.S. Supreme Court,
in *Douglas* v. *Jeannette,* 1943

ACKNOWLEDGMENTS

I am grateful to many people, both professionally and personally, who helped to give this book life.

I want to express my deep appreciation to Catherine Whitney for her invaluable advice and assistance in shaping the book, and for always being available and willing to share my concerns. Her ability and her optimism made this project possible.

My agent, Jane Dystel, was always a font of energy and enthusiasm. Her unflagging support was a great comfort in trying times.

Acknowledgments

My editor, Jonathan Karp, was always warmly encouraging and full of sensible and stimulating suggestions and ideas. It was a pleasure to work with him. I am also grateful to Harold Evans, whose vision and belief in me made this book a reality.

I am deeply grateful to my many friends and colleagues, particularly Nicholas Scoppetta, Marvin Frankel, Richard Heffner, Professor Milton Heumann, Professor James Jacobs, and Nancy Jacobs.

Throughout my career, countless men and women have lent their wisdom, support, and inspiration. I wish I had the space to thank them all. In writing the chapters in this book about the Fourth, Fifth, and Sixth Amendments, I have relied on the insights and scholarship of Professor Joseph D. Grano of Wayne State University Law School and Professor Craig M. Bradley of the Indiana University (Bloomington) School of Law.

Professor Grano's book, *Confessions, Truth and the Law* (University of Michigan Press, 1993), and Professor Bradley's book, *The Failure of the Criminal Procedure Revolution* (University of Pennsylvania Press, 1993), represent a brilliant culmination of their many years of research and writing in law reviews and journals. In my view, they are among the most insightful commentators on criminal procedure in the United States at this time. Those who wish to explore some of the themes in my book more deeply should read their work. In the discussion of the period leading up to the *Miranda* decision, I have also relied on the scholarship of Professor Gerald M. Caplan.

Acknowledgments

I wish to thank my secretary, Joanne Balecha, and my law secretary, Carol Schwartzkopf, for the good work they do for me every day. Special thanks to Lee Elkins, my previous law secretary, now a judge, for his many years of support.

Finally, my heartfelt thanks goes to my wife, Yona. Not only did she support and put up with me through this process, but she lent her substantial intellect and frank opinions to my writing. As always, Yona has been both my most valuable critic and most enthusiastic cheerleader.

CONTENTS

Contents

Guilty

THE PASSING PARADE
The View from the Bench

If you were to visit my courtroom on any given Wednesday, you would see the passing parade of our justice system as you have never seen it on television or in the movies. Wednesday is calendar day. That means there is no regular trial in session. On calendar day we try to dispose of cases, ready them for hearings and trials, and impose sentences in those cases where the defendant has been found guilty or has pleaded guilty. Today, there are ninety-four cases on the docket. I have the details of each one handwritten on an index card, and I begin arranging the cards across the desk according to their status. It's an old-fashioned system, but it has always served me well.

By 10:00 A.M., the courtroom is crowded, with an undercurrent of anxiety and urgency as deep as that in a busy hospital emergency room. Ninety-four cases means at least that many defendants, their families and friends, their victims, their lawyers. Most of the defendants are not out on bail. They're waiting for justice at the jail on Riker's Island, in the middle of New York's East River. They have been bused to the courthouse and are being kept in a holding cell on the twelfth floor. They'll be brought in as their names are called.

"Let's begin," I tell my clerk, Elizabeth. She calls a name and the players take their places for the first case of the day.

The DA speaks first. "The defendant is charged with selling five vials of crack cocaine to an undercover policeman. After his arrest, they found sixty-six vials on his person."

"Your honor." The defense attorney leans in sincerely. "My client absolutely denies it. He says it was a trap. He doesn't sell drugs."

"What about the sixty-six vials?" I ask—a fair question.

"He says he found them on the street," the attorney answers without a hint of guile.

"Found them?"

The attorney rolls his eyes and flashes a quick smile. We both know this probably isn't the truth.

"If he takes a plea, I can offer one year," I tell him.

The attorney goes back to the table and huddles with his client. They appear to be arguing. Finally, the attorney approaches the bench. "He wants to go to trial."

So we schedule a trial. In my opinion, the guy should have taken a plea. He's likely to be convicted at trial; the evidence is pretty conclusive. He'll get a higher sentence and cost the state more money in the process. But he has a right to a trial, and if that's what he wants, that's what he'll get.

The next case involves two young men barely out of their teens who are in my court for the first time. The men have been out on a low bail, and when their names are called, they swagger up to their seats and sit staring at me, their features blank and unconcerned. I suspect that their attorneys have already told them they'll probably get a light sentence, or even probation. They have that look about them.

"What's the charge?" I ask when the lawyers are standing before me.

"They are accused of stealing $18,000 worth of property from a UPS van on Sixteenth Street in the middle of the afternoon and loading the stuff into two waiting minivans," the DA says. "We're willing to offer six months and probation."

The defense attorneys are nodding. This seems good to them.

"Wait a minute. Why so light?" I ask the DA.

"Your honor, it was a onetime thing. Neither of these guys has ever been arrested before."

"A onetime thing." I ponder this statement. "Are you aware," I ask the attorneys, "that this is an organized crime scheme? These thefts happen all the time, in exactly this way."

"There's no evidence that these two are involved with an organized ring," one boy's attorney objects.

"Okay," I allow. "Help me out here. What do they do for a living? Do they have jobs?"

She fumbles with her papers. "Um . . . I don't know. I'll have to check."

"I see you've avoided the dangers of overpreparation," I chide her. "Do they have permanent addresses?"

"They're staying with friends."

"Where'd they get the vans? Vans are expensive. It says here that one van had Pennsylvania plates, and both were new, late-model vehicles."

"I don't know." She turns to her colleague, who shakes his head.

"No jobs, no permanent addresses." I glance at the boys, who are watching me closely from the defense table. "I can see that they're just the altar boys of the world."

I turn to the court officer. "Heads up on these two defendants, Sarge. They're both going in." The court officers stand behind the boys, who suddenly look very concerned.

"Here's my offer," I tell the attorneys. "State prison only, $10,000 bail each, one to three years. It's my final offer of the day. Tomorrow it will be higher."

The defense attorneys start to protest, but I wave them away. "Don't argue with me. Go explain to your clients what's going on and I'll call the case again this afternoon." The court officers are hustling the boys out of the room. Now their faces are registering shock and horror. A more appropriate reaction.

Some attorneys would rate my action as unnecessarily tough, given that the DA was willing to go with a lighter sentence. But it isn't my job to be a rubber stamp to whatever the attorneys suggest. I am constantly called upon to decide what's fair and right.

Our next case is the humor break for the morning. He's a guy with an ample supply of moxie. He has admitted to committing grand larceny—simultaneously collecting welfare from New York and New Jersey. Today, he's due for sentencing.

"Do you have anything you wish to say before I sentence you, sir?" I ask him.

The defendant rises to his feet and smiles at me pleasantly. "I have something for you to consider before sentencing," he says. "Your honor, I admit I stole money from the state, and I have burdened the state. That's why you shouldn't sentence me to prison. Incarcerating me would only cost the state more money, and I wouldn't want to do that."

"I'm sure you wouldn't." I smile back at him. "But why don't you let us worry about that." I sentence him to one to three years in jail.

And so it goes. One case followed by another. Often, the details are so similar we must fight not to make horror ordinary. I am aware every minute of the seriousness of what we do here. Sometimes, I look into the face of a defendant, a repeat offender who has been down this road many times before, and I shudder at the absence of remorse in his eyes. Other times, I feel compassion for a person who has been dealt a tough hand or was in the wrong place at the wrong time. And still other times, especially with the young, first offenders, addicts and the infirm, I try to avoid sending them to prison, if I can. But in every case, I strive to see each defendant as an individual, not a blurred mass—to look into each face and to study the facts.

The last case of the day is a sixty-eight-year-old Turkish limo driver who approaches the table, his face pasty white and his hands shaking. He speaks no English, so I summon a Turkish interpreter. (In New York the court clerk arranges for interpreters when needed.) I beckon the lawyers to the bench as I read the report.

"Your honor, this is a very sad case, an accident," the defense attorney says. "This poor old guy . . ."

"It says here he killed a woman with his car," I interrupt, scanning the report.

"Yes, but it was an accident."

The DA is silent. "What do you think?" I ask him.

He shrugs. "The People will agree to probation. He's sixty-eight years old and has never been in trouble with the law."

I sigh and look down at the limo driver hunched over the table. He seems to be crying. Indeed, it is a tragic situation. Death is tragic, and so is the reality that one rash act, one careless, thoughtless moment, can change so many lives. But I have to consider the facts. The limo driver had been parked illegally outside the Port Authority Bus Terminal building in mid-Manhattan, hoping to pick up a fare. It was five o'clock in the afternoon, a time when the streets and sidewalks are congested with a sea of commuters heading in all directions. A police officer tapped on the window and told him to move along. Rather than easing out into the barely moving traffic, our limo driver decided to take a shortcut via the sidewalk. He put his foot to the pedal and jumped the curb, plowing into a pedestrian and dragging her beneath the tires. Even then he didn't stop. He just kept going and was caught a few blocks away. The woman later died. The driver told the police he didn't know he'd hit anyone.

"A woman is dead," I say quietly. "A life has been taken. How can I justify probation?"

I struggle to resist the emotional appeal. The devastated limo driver. The faces of his family in the front row of benches. Everyone feels very sad that the elderly limo driver might go to prison. It would be tempting to let him off, just this once. But I can't do it. A woman is dead. There must be a relationship between the seriousness of the crime and the sentence that I impose. The limo driver recklessly caused the death of a pedestrian and then fled the scene. He was aware of the danger of what he was doing, and he consciously disregarded that risk. It would trivialize the seriousness of his acts to give him probation. It's tragic. But the limo driver is going to jail.

Knowing how to be a judge does not come automatically. It took me a good seven years to find my sea legs in this turbulent environment. That's because the law is not (as some believe) a clear-cut, objective set of rules where the judge serves merely as a rubber stamp. Life on the bench is far more relative than that.

When I was appointed a judge, I made a huge psychological leap from defense attorney and law professor. As it happened, my judicial mettle was challenged the very first day I put on a robe.

The first case brought before me that first morning seemed very straightforward. It involved a sixteen-year-old boy who was charged with throwing an elderly woman to the ground and stealing her purse. It was my task to make a decision about bail. I studied the papers and asked questions. The boy was young, he had no prior arrests, and his parents were sitting behind him in the courtroom looking responsible and concerned.

There is really only one reason for bail: to assure that the defendant returns to court. It's not meant to be punitive. So, even though the young man's alleged crime was serious, my real concern when deciding bail was whether or not he would return to court or simply disappear, slipping through the sieve of the city. Looking at his clean record and his stalwart parents, I decided that he was a good risk, and I paroled him.

The young man did return—unfortunately, not in the way I expected. Two days later, he was arrested again for robbing another woman on the street. I was quite upset, and I felt a twinge of self-doubt and some responsibility for this latest victim. Obviously, if I had not paroled the boy, he wouldn't have been back on the street and wouldn't have robbed another woman. I glimpsed at that moment the heavy burden of being a judge, and realized that there are consequences to every decision.

More troubling, the young man was represented by a civil liberties attorney who happened to be a good friend of mine. He was quite skillful, with a sharp knowledge of the law, and he reminded me that as bad as the second arrest looked, the bail facts were essentially the same.

"The bail facts may be the same, but the bail *factors* are not," I said. "Now he's got two charges and he's facing more time."

The lawyer argued persuasively and I believed correctly that the second arrest should not be a consideration in the bail matter, and I let the young man go a second time.

Three days later, there he was again, back in my courtroom, having been arrested for yet another robbery. That was it. "In you go!" I declared, wishing in retrospect that I had sent him in after the second robbery.

This incident troubled me greatly. It didn't seem like a very auspicious start to my career as a judge. I pondered my decision, my beliefs about the appropriateness of bail, my feelings about being on the bench, and I feared that I might have been affected by the fact that the defense attorney was a former colleague of mine from the Civil Liberties Union and he had made me question my own beliefs. A chill ran through me as I realized how fragile the balance of justice really is. We are, after all, merely human beings with human inclinations. Yet in our hands is the life and liberty of the people.

I resolved from that day on to try and put aside such feelings, to deafen myself to the roars of disapproval. I couldn't allow myself to weaken every time someone in my courtroom felt disappointed or betrayed or disagreed with me. In that circumstance, I was the one whose job it was to decide. Being wishy-washy was certain folly.

A judge doesn't have to be superhuman, but I learned one thing: Since there are two sides in every courtroom scenario, it is impossible to satisfy everyone. Nor can a judge be overly worried about how people will respond to him. That doesn't mean he should be indifferent. But somehow he should find a way to keep his personal feelings in check.

In the seventeenth century, Sir Edward Coke, chief justice of the King's Bench in England, once said, "A judge ceaseth to have friends." That's an overstatement—at least, I hope it is!—but sometimes it seems like the truth. When a judge mounts the bench, he leaves his relationships behind.

I have been a judge now for twenty-five years, and I know I have a reputation for being tough. Around Centre Street, some lawyers even refer to me as "the Prince of Darkness," and it is well known that many defense attorneys are loathe to appear before me.

Few people meeting me today would readily say I am idealistic, although I am driven by idealism. I was always driven by idealism.

When I was a kid growing up in Brooklyn, my idol was Clarence Darrow. He was a fighter against oppression and injustice. He defended people who were downtrodden and whose liberty was at stake. To me, there was nothing better in the world than being a defense attorney.

The inspiration for this passion was my mother. She was very strong and controlling, very clear about what she wanted. I loved my mother, but I reacted to her firm grip in the predictable manner of young people. I challenged her authority, just to see if I could, to establish my own style and independence.

But even though my mother was controlling, my family was loving. So while I fought against authority, I didn't hate it. I learned early on that authority could be benevolent. You could respect it and still question it. This understanding evolved into a passion for the law, and particularly for being a defense attorney. As an attorney, it was my mandate to fight against authority when it was overbearing, abusive, or unjust, but also to respect and believe in the system. When I challenged the system it was not from disrespect; rather, it was the ultimate form of respect.

I understood then, as I do today, that absent challenge, authority becomes totalitarian. Authority needs to be challenged if we are to ensure the integrity of the process. It is one of the great truths of our system.

The law is wonderful work. I've always told my children how great it is to be able to get up in the morning and look forward to the day. The criminal law is where society and the individual meet as adversaries—with liberty and even life at stake. Could anything be more dramatic or interesting than such a confrontation? And not only is it interesting in that philosophical, governmental sense. It's intellectually exciting and emotionally powerful. The human drama, the passing parade, is completely engaging.

It is precisely because I love the law so much that I have decided to write this book. In the same way that a doctor shows love by turning his patients' lives upside down, by carving out diseased cells, by being fully honest even when the news is bad—that is precisely how we in the law must set about curing our system.

Everyone says that lawyers can't resist a good fight. I dare to say that this is the fight of our lives.

| 1 |

ANYTHING BUT THE TRUTH

Truth Undermined by "Fairness"— and Criminals Go Free

How dreadful knowledge of the truth can be when there's no help in truth!
SOPHOCLES, *Oedipus Rex*

If a man can rob, he can lie.
MY MOTHER

On Christmas Eve 1968, ten-year-old Pamela Powers was attending an event with her family at the Des Moines, Iowa, YMCA. She excused herself to go to the bathroom and never came back.

About half an hour after Pamela left her family, several people saw a man leave the YMCA building carrying a blanket-wrapped bundle, which he placed on the front seat of his car. A boy who helped him open the door (his hands were full) told police he "saw two legs in it and they were skinny and white."

The police suspected that the bundle contained Pamela's body, but the suspect was already gone, heading across Iowa on Interstate 80. Police later found his car abandoned in Davenport, 160 miles away, containing heartbreaking evidence—the blanket and some of Pamela's clothing.

Two days later, a man named Robert Williams telephoned Henry McKnight, a Des Moines lawyer, because he knew the police were looking for him. On McKnight's advice he surrendered to the Davenport police. A judge ordered that he be transported back to Des Moines.

Des Moines police captain Leaming and another officer drove to Davenport to collect Williams, with a warning from McKnight: "Don't talk to him. Don't question him. He's represented by counsel now; he's been arraigned; so you mustn't talk to him." The officers nodded. They knew the law full well. Once a defendant had been arraigned and was represented, the police couldn't question him outside the presence of his attorney.

They started off on the 160-mile journey to Des Moines. As they drove, it began to snow, and midway through the trip, the snow was coming down very hard and piling up along the road.

Captain Leaming was aware he could not question Williams, but he also knew that Williams was a fragile man of conscience—an escaped mental patient with strong religious tendencies. Very casually, Leaming turned to Williams and said, "Reverend Williams, you know I'm not supposed to question you and I'm not going to question you. But I have something I want to mention. It's a concern of mine. Just think about what I'm saying, but don't respond, please." And he went on.

"It's snowing like crazy, as you can see, and pretty soon the ground will be covered over with snow. It's Christmastime. I'm sure this family would like to have a good Christian burial for their child. I guess, if you don't know where the child is, there's no point in me even mentioning it. But if you do, it's probably your last chance to give this family a Christian burial for their daughter. Don't say anything. I just want you to think about that."

Some hours later, as the car approached Des Moines, Williams said, "Okay, let me take you to the body." And he took them to the place where he had buried Pamela in a ditch about two miles off the interstate. Scientific evidence showed that Pamela had been sexually assaulted and smothered.

Williams was convicted of the murder of Pamela Powers, and the state courts affirmed Williams's conviction. The federal court, however, concluded that Captain Leaming had violated Williams's rights by speaking to him outside the presence of his attorney, and the court ordered a new trial. When the state appealed to the U.S. Supreme Court, many people thought the Court would take this opportunity to overrule or at least limit the controversial *Miranda* doctrine. Instead, the majority opinion by Justice Potter Stewart stated that Leaming's "Christian burial speech" had indeed violated Williams's rights, since his attorney had made it clear to police that Williams wouldn't answer any questions. In a new trial, Williams's de facto confession—the fact that he led officers to Pamela's body—would be suppressed.

Although Williams's case would be argued and reargued in the courts for many years to come (including yet a second decision to overturn the conviction), there was never any real doubt that he committed the crime. There was no police abuse, coercion, or even questioning. He wasn't threatened. Captain Leaming simply made an appeal to his conscience, to his decency as a religious man. And Williams responded.

The remarkable thing about this case was that so much concern was shown for Captain Leaming's speech and so little concern was given to punishing the murderer of Pamela Powers.

Sadly, this is where we've come: the point where a man who has committed a terrible wrong may not try to cleanse his conscience. There is no respect for the truth. And I challenge you to find the justice.

We want to believe that the search for justice walks hand in hand with the search for truth, and surely our courts pay lip service to that value. Every day, in thousands of courtrooms across America, lawyers stand before judges and juries and proclaim, "We are not afraid of the truth." With utmost sincerity they promise, "We are here to seek the truth." O. J. Simpson's attorney Johnnie Cochran could look downright pious when he spoke of his concern for the truth. But every day he and his colleagues skimmed the edge of ethics to paint elaborate theories that strained an ordinary person's judgment and common sense.

In reality, the law is not necessarily a search for the truth. Indeed, it is often *not* a search for the truth. Our system is a carefully crafted maze, constructed of elaborate and impenetrable barriers to the truth. Even when the evidence against the accused is as clear as a ringing bell, lawyers will grasp at anything to fog the issues and mask the terrible facts.

Last year I had a case that seemed, on the face of it, to be pretty clear-cut. Curtis Dickson shot his girlfriend Lisa eight times in the back. The shooting occurred in a very public spot, in full view of many witnesses. There was never any real question that he did it.

But it's at that very point that the game began.

These are the facts: Curtis and Lisa had been living together for about nine years, but it was, by all accounts, a tumultuous relationship. There was some evidence that cocaine might have been involved. Then, two months before the shooting, Lisa moved out of their apartment and told Curtis that she was ending the relationship for good. Curtis, however, wasn't content to let her go. He kept trying to win her back and was furious when he heard she might be seeing another man.

One day, Curtis picked Lisa up at work and she agreed to let him drive her to the Bronx, where she wanted to do some shopping. As they moved slowly through rush-hour traffic, he berated Lisa about her dating another man. Lisa became fed up with his attitude, and she started to get out of the car. The location was Forty-first Street and Eighth Avenue, across from the Port Authority Bus Terminal, a crowded place at that time of day.

As Lisa began to step out the door, Curtis pulled a gun and shot her twice in the back. She fell facedown in the middle of the gutter, close to the intersection. Curtis then rolled the car a few feet forward, into the intersection, and jumped out. Grabbing Lisa roughly by the back of her neck, Curtis pulled her up and pumped six more shots into her back. Then he put the gun underneath his jacket, got back in the car, and drove it to a nearby roadway reserved for taxi cabs. He left the car there and fled the scene.

Over the next two hours, Curtis placed numerous calls to Lisa's mother saying that he'd killed her daughter. He sobbed into the phone, "I'm sorry . . . I'm sorry . . . I killed her. I'm so sorry." Lisa's mother didn't believe him. She kept hanging up.

She only learned the truth when two police officers arrived at her apartment with news of her daughter's death. "Curtis did it! He said he did it!" she wailed. The police set up a phone tap, and the next morning they captured Curtis on tape once again confessing to the murder.

That very morning, Curtis surrendered himself to the police precinct and made a five-page written statement. He was also identified in a lineup by several people who had witnessed the shooting. It was never disputed that he shot and killed Lisa.

Even so, his lawyer was determined to make a defense. He chose the only defense really available—insanity—and he started to line up psychiatrists to testify that Curtis didn't know what he was doing.

Maybe you're thinking that the insanity defense was legitimate. After all, would a sane person shoot his girlfriend eight times in the back? But in a courtroom, insanity is not a medical concept. We define it in a cognitive way: Did he understand what he was doing? Did he understand that it was wrong? If he understood one or the other, he'd be criminally responsible. If he didn't understand either, he could be found legally insane.

Insanity is not, as many people believe, a matter of irresistible impulse. It's not a loss of control—as in, "I was so upset, I lost my head." Rather, it's a loss of cognition.

It would be the jury's task to decide if Curtis was legally insane when he fired the first two bullets, and still insane when he fired six more. They ruled against insanity, and eventually Curtis was convicted of murder in the second degree. I was satisfied with the verdict. I thought it was a terrible crime and Curtis deserved to be sentenced to the maximum, and that's what I did.

It looked as though justice had been done, but I felt uneasy about the whole process. For one thing, in order to get past the layers of obfuscation and discover the truth—that Curtis was a murderer and not an insane person—we had to undergo lengthy hearings, ridiculously contrived psychiatric testimony, and endless motions by the defense attorney who went to great lengths to delay and defeat the eventual result. And once the taxpayers' money had been generously used for this purpose over the long weeks of the trial, that wasn't even the end of it. Soon the case of Curtis Dickson will be appearing in an appeals court near you for another go at the system. It's a demoralizing process, especially when you're dealing with a man whose guilt was never in doubt.

Of course, it must be noted that the search for truth is not our only task. Even if there is evidence that a defendant committed a crime, the state cannot violate his rights in the process of prosecuting him. We live in a democracy, not a police state. And even when a defendant has shown on numerous occasions in the past that he is not averse to flaunting the law and endangering his fellow citizens, he still has the same rights as every law-abiding citizen of the United States, because in America we have placed controls on excessive governmental authority. The entire thrust of our Bill of Rights is to restrain governmental power and, ideally, to allow it to operate effectively, without oppression and abuse. So, we limit truth in the interest of fairness and restraint.

Our courts struggle with the implications of this tension, and we long for equal measures of truth and fairness—the ideological balance of scales that is the basis of justice. Far too often, we are disappointed.

In twenty-five years on the bench in the heart of New York City, I feel as though I've seen it all. My job is to stand at the center of the adversarial system and try to keep the scales in balance. When a man appears before me accused of a crime, the ball is literally in my court. I have to make sure that everything that preceded his appearance was done according to law. But often, as my court day grows burdened beneath the onslaught of files and motions and hearings, I long to hear an answer to the one question that rarely gets asked or answered: Did you do it?

As we take this journey through the system together, you'll discover that, in itself, the limitation on truth-seeking isn't such a bad thing, since we hold other values as well in a free society. But I hope you will also begin to question whether the weight of other considerations has actually made truth subordinate and even irrelevant.

There is a growing concern in America that criminal trials, despite being surrounded by extensive procedural protections, too often produce results that are inaccurate or unjust. As I was writing this book, the O. J. Simpson trial was slowly grinding along, well into its ninth month—not counting the months of preliminary hearings that preceded it. When the trial began and Judge Lance Ito ruled that it would be televised, we all thought, "Aha! This is wonderful. It will serve as a lesson in the criminal justice system. The world will see why our system of justice is better than any other." By now, most people feel ashamed of the process they witnessed. It may have been as interesting as a soap opera, but it was not an effective way to administer justice. The Simpson trial aired the dirty laundry of our courts for the world to see. It was lengthy, convoluted, regularly subjected to trickery and bickering among attorneys, and seemingly focused on every question imaginable except the question, Did the defendant murder two people?

We have a system that is so perplexing and so prolonged that it is not meaningfully available to about 90 percent of those who are subjected to it. Even if the Simpson trial had been a perfectly run case, it would still represent only one case out of many thousands. It should be clear to anyone with a minimal grasp of mathematics that if one criminal trial takes a year, thousands of other cases are relegated to the dust heap. And the more complex and overburdened our system becomes, the less truth comes out.

Only thirty-five years ago, our criminal justice system was relatively simple: A person was arrested, indicted, and tried. But life in the courts is no longer that simple.

I am often amazed at the manner in which the system chugs along in blatant disregard of that simple fact. Recently, I had a man come before me who was serving twenty-five years to life for murder. Along with his murder charge there had also been a drug charge, and now the DA wanted to bring up that charge.

"Why are we spending time on this?" I asked impatiently. "He's not going anywhere. He's already in jail for twenty-five years." I was frustrated because there were ninety other cases on the docket that day, and this seemed a low priority. I guess the best answer to why the DA brought up the drug charge is because it was there. It was not part of an overall strategy on the part of the DA's office. It had no practical meaning to the pursuit of justice.

It also distresses me that our public officials constantly act in ways that show a total lack of awareness of how burdened our system is. They call for more cops on the street and more prisons because these are popular symbols to show that the officials are "tough on crime." But you rarely hear anyone talk about putting more money into the system that is supposed to process the increased number of criminals being arrested.

The day is eight hours long, and there are only so many judges and so many courtrooms. And even when we make an honest effort to expedite a case, we can't predict the boulders that are going to roll across the road without warning. For example, say on a given day my task at hand is to charge a jury. In order for me to do the first thing—to even say, "Good morning, ladies and gentlemen of the jury"—everybody has to be there. The defendant, the lawyers from both sides, the court officers, the clerk, the court reporter, all of the jurors, and myself. If anybody is late, we all sit and wait. We're paralyzed.

Our system of justice is exquisite, and it would be wonderful except that it's been designed for bargain-basement justice. It's a crowded marketplace, yet we treat it as though we have the luxury of a leisurely ramble through the halls of a private showroom.

At the same time, we have established statutes that give defendants the right to a speedy trial. These statutes establish a rule that says if we don't go to trial within a certain period, the case will be dismissed without regard to its merits or how dangerous the criminal might be. The speedy trial statute is a mathematical calculation that renders the quest for truth irrelevant.

Let's be frank about this. The long arm of the law is somewhat fractured these days. Because of the volume, we don't arrest everybody we can. Many of the people who are arrested in less serious cases are given desk appearances. We let them go and give them a date to come back. A large percentage of them never come back, and warrants are issued. There are 500,000 open warrants at this time in New York City. We defeat truth because we make an arrest and then let the person go, knowing we'll probably never see him again.

Even if we do catch up with him, maybe it's two or three years later when the witnesses are gone, the evidence is stale, and nobody remembers what the case is about. Volume affects the truth-finding process.

I think most citizens would shudder to know how many criminals have never showed up in court to face justice. And you might well ask, Why don't we demand that the police find them and bring them in? Well, we could do that if there were enough police. But even if we pulled in all the outstanding cases, the sheer volume would require that we send most of them right back out onto the street.

Even when an accused person is brought to trial, there is no guarantee that the process will lead to truth-seeking. Any defense attorney worth his salt will make the case a test of strength, not truth. He might try to exclude prior statements the defendant has made to the police, property that was seized, or other evidence. He might challenge the initial identification and arrest. These motions are based on "exclusionary rules" derived from the U.S. Supreme Court's interpretation of the Fourth, Fifth, and Sixth Amendments. In New York, there are currently between twenty and thirty exclusionary rules under which evidence might be suppressed.

Not all of the exclusionary rules burden the search for truth. Some inquire into the reliability and voluntariness of a confession, or the reliability of an identification. But with many of the exclusionary rules, we are dealing with unquestionably reliable and highly probative evidence; when we exclude it, we are hampering the fact finders (the judge or jury) in their quest of the full truth.

The defense attorney can also try to exclude evidence that was obtained in violation of a "privilege"—attorney-client, husband-wife, doctor-patient. I don't question these relational privileges; I only question the length to which the courts have liberally interpreted them. I can appreciate the need for zones of privacy and confidentiality, but we should also be aware of their cost to the truth-seeking process.

If the facts related to these motions are in dispute—and they usually are—the court must hold hearings. These hearings can be quite prolonged. In some cases, the pretrial hearings are longer than the trial itself. They often have nothing to do with whether the defendant is innocent or guilty. Indeed, hearings can often reveal that a defendant *is* guilty, which is why he's so eager to suppress evidence. But the central issue, *Did he do it?,* is the last question we ask—and sometimes, when evidence is suppressed, we don't even ask it at all.

I recently tried a robbery case with a very competent and conscientious defense attorney. The defendant was charged with robbing a Belgian tourist in mid-Manhattan while the tourist was on a three-hour layover at Kennedy Airport on his way home. After he gave his name, address, and phone number to police, the tourist caught his plane and flew to Belgium.

The case was able to go forward because at the time of the robbery the defendant was being followed by plainclothes policemen who observed the entire incident.

The tourist refused to return from Belgium for the trial, and the defense attorney sought a "missing witness charge"—an instruction that the failure to produce the witness would permit the jury to infer that the witness if called would not support the district attorney's case.

During the argument, the defense attorney admitted that she had telephoned the witness in Belgium, that he had confirmed being robbed, and that he'd confirmed that the defendant was the robber.

"Doesn't your own statement belie the inference you're seeking?" I asked.

"It does," she agreed. "But my client is entitled to it." In other words, her client was entitled to mislead the jury—and this has increasingly become the most sacred of a defendant's rights.

When it is proper to say in a court of law that a defendant is *entitled* to mislead a jury, you have to wonder.

We also have discovery rules. These were originally intended to aid in the search for truth, but it doesn't really work that way because discovery is not entirely reciprocal. The discovery statutes require the prosecution to turn over all of its files and information to the defendant's attorney, but in most jurisdictions the defendant's attorney does not have the same obligation. There's a reason for this. It is, after all, the DA who has the burden of proof. Unfortunately, that absence of full reciprocal disclosure contributes to perjury and witness intimidation. Once the defense knows what the prosecution's evidence is, he may build his case around refuting it. In this way, discovery may impede the truth, not further it. The typical scene goes something like this:

"I wasn't there."

"We have a video . . ."

"Okay, I was there, but it was self-defense."

"The victim had no weapon."

"Okay, I did it, but I was crazy."

The defendant literally crafts his story from the details of the prosecution's case.

Finally, we have the privilege against self-incrimination. That means the defendant, the very person who may know the most about the case, cannot be required to tell his version of the story. And his failure to testify cannot be commented on. The judge must tell the jury that it may draw no adverse inference from the fact that the defendant did not testify. I think this is an unfair limitation on the pursuit of justice. It angered me tremendously when I presided over the Joel Steinberg trial several years ago. I'll tell you that story later. It is a sterling example of decency and truth being sidetracked.

In the adversary system of American justice, the judge controls the courtroom, but he does not control the trial. He is passive. If we were in Europe, it would be a different matter. Judges in the Continental systems have extensive files available to them. They are intimately familiar with the evidence, and they initiate and conduct most of the questioning of witnesses.

The American judge, on the other hand, is fearful of intervening, often uninformed about the details of the case, and unable to comment on the evidence. His errors will be closely scrutinized by appellate courts. In America, it is the lawyers, not the judge, who organize the trial and ask the questions.

For the most part, judges are recruited from the ranks of trial lawyers—as opposed to European systems, where judging is a separate career. Our state judges are appointed or elected for fixed terms that require them to be sufficiently popular or politically connected to maintain their position. Since the trial bar has significant input in this process, that might be a factor in determining judges' willingness to meaningfully control the behavior or misbehavior of the lawyers who appear before them.

In the Continental systems, the lawyers play only a supplemental role. It is the court that takes the lead in inquiring after the facts and has the responsibility for reaching accurate and reliable results. In our adversary system, the attorneys are well informed, the judge is inert, and the jury is passive and receptive, basing its decision only on what it is given. Evidence not produced by the attorneys is therefore never known by the decision makers.

The judge is also a target of the defense attorney. If his client is convicted, the defense attorney hopes to win a reversal on appeal by showing that the trial judge has made legal errors. I'll tell you quite frankly that it is a terrible feeling to have a conviction reversed on appeal because of an error you supposedly made. The implications of knowing you contributed to the release of a vicious criminal can keep you awake at night. But I learned early on in my career that if you try to tiptoe through the process, fearful of error, the results are equally disastrous. A judge's job is to be decisive. That's what we get paid for. Judging is deciding.

Every ruling a judge makes is a potential weapon for the defense on appeal. And the rulings are often instantaneous responses to questions that arise suddenly and without warning. A demand for swift rulings is compelling because a judge normally does not want to distract and delay the jury and destroy continuity.

And if a defendant is convicted, there is a whole universe of opportunities to appeal. The court of appeals is *really* a gamble. As I sometimes tell my law students, "The court of appeals is in session; we are all in danger."

A trial is a minefield, and any judicial misstep—or even a perceived misstep—can lead to a reversal of the verdict, with no consideration of whether the defendant is guilty or not.

In theory, the court of appeals prevents the accused from being railroaded. It protects citizens against neglectful judges, lazy or inept lawyers, or the use of illegal force by the state. In reality, it often operates as a lottery. The outcome is rarely determined by a unanimous agreement on the meaning and execution of the law. The process is rarely about truth. The question isn't, Did he do it? or even, Did the state prove its case?

So, we are left to ask, what is the possibility of justice without truth? Does it not become a pointless exercise if truth is so subordinated that the likelihood of its emerging is remote?

What are we here for? Why do we show up in court every day if not to find the truth?

Let us remember that legal procedure is a means, not an end. Therefore, the purpose of procedure should be to enhance the law, not to delay or defeat the law's intention. I believe it stands to reason that a primary objective of procedural rules should be to facilitate the discovery of truth.

The function of the criminal process is to determine guilt with a view toward imposing a penalty. When the innocent are convicted or the guilty are set free, the substantive law is defeated. That's why truth must be a primary goal of criminal procedure. Indeed, truth must be the goal of *any* rational procedural system. Although reasonable people may disagree about the best way to determine the truth of a matter, no reasonable person would advocate a procedural system that makes the truth *more* difficult.

The Founders started off with a Bill of Rights that sought to be the most civilized document in the world. They designed it to be the apex of human understanding of how governments should interact with their citizens.

We know from our history that we have to control government. The American Revolution arose from that belief. But it's not such a simple concept. How do you control government in such a way that allows it to play its proper role while its citizens live free lives?

Our Founding Fathers debated this question and they came up with the Constitution as representing their best judgment about how to do it. And clearly, it was a tremendous advance over the system of arbitrarily throwing people in jail because you didn't approve of them.

The Constitution and its implications have been the subject of serious thought and debate for two hundred years, and we're still grappling with it. The proper tension between government and the individual is an issue that will never go away.

Yet although this is a rich and complex area of discussion, I am distressed by the fact that in the final years of the twentieth century we have ceased to argue effectively about it. Instead, we've learned to take a lot of it as a given, as the apotheosis of human learning and understanding that cannot any longer be questioned. But that's nonsense. Of course it should be questioned! And if you question it and decide things should stay as they are, okay. And if you question it and come up with a better way, that's okay, too. There's no harm done in questioning.

It is my opinion that many of our laws and statutes are illogical and arbitrary. We need some straight talking about these issues, but it's hard to find the forum where honest dialogue can take place.

Even in the law journals, arguably the center of legal learning and dialogue, there has been little attempt to view the system as a whole. A law review article might discuss the Fifth Amendment, or the Fourth Amendment, or the Sixth Amendment, but there is no attempt to integrate these various standards—to make a fair, honest, and just *whole* out of a painfully fragmented system.

The irony is that change is inherent in the law. The law cries out to us to challenge every detail, to avoid rigidity, to question every firm notion, attitude, and belief. It demands that we be skeptical of the very principles we hold most dear, even as we strive to fulfill their tenets. We are meant to squirm when issues of life and liberty are at stake.

When I was a fresh, young defense attorney, one of my first cases was a man who was charged with robbery. I took my job as his advocate very seriously. During that period, I was visiting my mother and I proudly told her, "I'm representing a man accused of robbery."

She frowned. "What did he do?"

"He's *charged* with robbing an old man coming home from a store," I told her.

She looked at me with horror, and I could see the pride in her son the lawyer quickly slipping away. "How can you represent a man like that?"

I explained patiently. "Well, Mom, he tells me he's not guilty."

My mother gazed at me pityingly, as though I was the most naive creature on earth, and said with a sigh, "Son, if he can rob, he can lie."

I often think of my mother's words on that day. They serve as my reminder, a tickler to my conscience. Even the most sacred idea is open to scrutiny. And even as we search for truth, we all too often give credence to a lie.

| 2 |

SNOWY NIGHTS AND CARS ON THE RUN

The Fourth Amendment and the Suppression of Evidence

The law of search and seizure is intolerably confusing.
JUSTICE LEWIS POWELL,
U.S. Supreme Court,
Robbins v. California

Pamela Mason* was fourteen years old—a bright, industrious girl who lived with her mother and younger brother in Manchester, New Hampshire. To earn extra money, Pamela baby-sat after school and in the evenings, advertising her services on the bulletin board of a local Laundromat.

On January 13, the weather was bitter cold, with the threat of a storm hanging in the air. By the time Pamela arrived home

---

* The cases described in this book are real; the young victims here and in chapter 1 were both named Pamela.

from school at 4:15, it was snowing heavily—winds gusting the snow into huge drifts. In many parts of the country, such a storm would have halted all normal activity. But the people of Manchester were used to this; they went on with their business.

When Pamela walked in the door, her mother was preparing to leave for her waitressing job at a nearby restaurant. She told Pamela that a man had called looking for a baby-sitter that evening, and he had promised to call back. She kissed Pamela and her brother good-bye and left the house.

At 4:30, the phone rang. Pamela's younger brother, who answered the call but did not overhear the conversation, later reported that the caller was a man. After the call, Pamela prepared dinner for her brother and herself and left the house soon after 6:00 P.M. Her family never again saw her alive.

Eight days later, Pamela's frozen body was discovered in a snowdrift beside an interstate highway a few miles from her home. Her throat had been slashed and she had been shot in the head. Medical evidence showed that Pamela had died sometime between 8:00 and 10:00 P.M. on the night she disappeared.

A manhunt ensued. Two witnesses told police that at 9:30 P.M. on the night of the murder, they had stopped to offer assistance to a man in a 1951 Pontiac that was stopped on the highway near where Pamela's body was found. The 1951 Pontiac became a crucial lead in the case.

Edward Coolidge came under suspicion seven days after the body was found. His 1951 Pontiac matched the description of the witnesses, and one of his neighbors told police that Coolidge had been absent from his home between 5:00 and 11:00 P.M. on the night of the murder.

The police first talked to Coolidge at his home on the evening of January 28—fifteen days after Pamela was killed. They arranged for him to come to the station the following Sunday to answer more questions. During that questioning, Coolidge told the police that he had been shopping in a nearby town at the time of the murder. He also told them he was a frequent customer at the Laundromat where Pamela had posted her baby-sitting notice and had been there the day of the murder. Incidentally, he admitted to having committed an unrelated larceny and was held overnight in connection with that offense, but was released the following day.

While Coolidge was being questioned at the police station, two officers went to his home and talked with his wife. They asked whether Coolidge owned firearms, and his wife produced two shotguns and two rifles, which she voluntarily gave to the police.

The evidence against Coolidge was beginning to mount. Investigators located a knife near the Laundromat—later determined to belong to Coolidge—that could have inflicted Pamela's stab wounds. And the criminal investigation laboratory concluded that one of the firearms given to the police by Coolidge's wife had fired the bullet found in Pamela's brain.

Furthermore, police learned that Coolidge had contacted four different persons before Pamela's body had been found in an attempt to fabricate an alibi for the night of her murder.

On February 19, more than one month after the crime, the evidence against Coolidge was presented to the state attorney general, who was authorized under New Hampshire law to issue arrest and search warrants. Based on the evidence, the attorney general issued a warrant for Coolidge's arrest and four search warrants—including one for the search and seizure of Coolidge's 1951 Pontiac.

That day, police officers went to Coolidge's home and placed him under arrest. They took charge of his Pontiac, which was parked in the driveway, and two hours later it was towed to the police station.

During the search of the Pontiac, the police obtained vacuum sweepings of dirt and other fine particles that matched particles taken from Pamela's clothing. Experts testified that based on the sweepings they could conclude that Pamela had been in Coolidge's car.

Was ever a case so clear?

Coolidge was found guilty of murder and sentenced to life in prison. No one was surprised. The evidence against him was great; the prosecution was able to establish a direct link between him and the girl on the night in question. But after the verdict, Coolidge's lawyers appealed, as lawyers normally do, and the case eventually went to the U.S. Supreme Court.

The basis of the appeal was not that the police had acted improperly. They were very meticulous about gathering evidence, and that evidence was irrefutable. Not only did they have a search warrant but they had probable cause for the search warrant. Every step of the way, they checked and double-checked. They wanted to be absolutely sure that the perpetrator of this horrible crime was sent away.

So what was the problem with the prosecution's case? The problem was that in New Hampshire, the attorney general for the state was, for purposes of issuing warrants, considered a judicial officer, and it was the attorney general who issued the warrant. The Supreme Court, however, held that the attorney general of the state of New Hampshire was a law enforcement officer and not a judicial officer, regardless of what the New Hampshire law said. Law enforcement officers were not qualified to issue warrants. Based on that technicality—that the attorney general was not a legitimate issuer of warrants—Coolidge's conviction was set aside and the matter was returned to the New Hampshire courts for retrial.

The issue was not the legality of the search. Nor was it the legality of the original retrieval of guns from Coolidge's wife. The deliverance of justice to a man guilty of a most heinous crime hinged on a mere technicality unrelated to these more substantive concerns.

Although Coolidge's crime was a horrible one, and the conduct of the police could not have been more restrained or professional, the criminal went free because the constable blundered in the eyes of the U.S. Supreme Court. There was a total lack of proportionality. Coolidge was the recipient of a bonanza in our criminal justice sweepstakes. He won the lottery when he persuaded the Court to overlook his horrible acts and focus on a minor good-faith error by the police.

This case happened more than twenty years ago, but it rattles me every time I think about it. Did I become a judge for this? Is this the system I am proud to be a part of? The Coolidge reversal makes me ashamed.

Stories like this are an insult to common sense and fair play. There is certainly little feeling for the victim, who was brutally tortured and murdered. There is also little feeling for the *truth*.

If you're looking for the major culprit in the malaise-ridden judicial system, for the kink in the works that practically guarantees justice will not be done, look at the convoluted way the Courts have interpreted the Fourth Amendment.

Essentially, the Fourth Amendment asserts a right to be free of unreasonable searches by the government. It states: "The right of the people to be secure in their persons, houses, papers, and effects, against unreasonable searches and seizures, shall not be violated, and no warrants shall issue, but upon probable cause, supported by oath or affirmation, and particularly describing the place to be searched, and the persons or things to be seized." And out of this premise we have created what is called the exclusionary rule—that is, evidence obtained in violation of the Fourth Amendment should be excluded from a criminal trial.

Few would disagree that in the United States, police officers should not be allowed to just burst into your home, or search your car, or rifle through your handbag on a whim. Such behavior would betray our fundamental right to be protected from unreasonable government interference with our lives. But we've gotten ourselves into a hopeless morass with the Fourth Amendment. Day by day, case by case, the results become more ridiculous and more difficult to understand and predict. The bottom line: Criminals are going free.

I don't mean *alleged* criminals. I'm not referring to *innocent* men and women who were arrested by mistake or because of false evidence. I'm talking about people who are clearly criminals. There's no issue about the reliability of the evidence against them. But that evidence is often completely thrown out because of some technical mistake made in the course of the arrest.

You may think that in the interest of protecting civil rights, that's fair. The problem is, the law is so muddy that the police can't find out what they are allowed to do even if they wanted to. If a street cop took a sabbatical and holed himself up in a library for six months doing nothing but studying the law on search and seizure, he wouldn't know any more than he did before he started. The law is totally confusing, yet we expect cops to always know at every moment what the proper action is. It's no wonder that police officers are somewhat edgy—especially when they're pursuing cases involving vicious murderers and rapists.

How is it that the Fourth Amendment has been interpreted in such a way that a man like Coolidge, who was known to have committed one of the worst crimes imaginable, could be freed? Supreme Court Justice Hugo Black wondered that himself when he wrote in *Coolidge:* "The Fourth Amendment prohibits unreasonable searches and seizures. The Amendment says nothing about consequences. It certainly nowhere provides for the exclusion of evidence as the remedy for violation." Black is correct. The Fourth Amendment does not state that illegally obtained evidence must be excluded. We've come to that point entirely on our own.

Today, the exclusionary rule is so much a part of our legal landscape that it's hard to believe that it wasn't required in the states prior to 1961. Not until 172 years after the adoption of the Fourth Amendment did the U.S. Supreme Court first impose it on the states.

Supporters of the exclusionary rule cannot point to a single major statement from the time of the Founding Fathers—or even the Reconstruction era—supporting Fourth Amendment exclusion of evidence in a criminal trial. Indeed, in the century after our nation's independence, the *idea* of exclusion seemed so illogical that it was almost never raised by criminal defendants.

That is not to say that the end justifies the means. When police officers clearly violate the law, there must be meaningful sanctions. A balance must be maintained between being fair and being effective. But as you will see, the exclusionary rule as it is presently designed does not contain such beautiful logic.

The exclusionary rule, as binding on the states, resulted from the 1961 case of Dollree Mapp, an Ohio landlady. But the road to the *Mapp* decision reaches back farther. Prior to the twentieth century, there were few rumblings about the allowability of evidence seized in a search. But in the twentieth century, several cases were decided that made the validity of the search a factor in the admissibility of evidence presented at trial. Before the *Mapp* case, however, the Supreme Court had never said that evidence obtained illegally by the states must be excluded altogether.

Judges are not infallible—even Supreme Court justices. But we would hope that their decisions are thoughtful, reasonable, and well argued. The tragedy of the *Mapp* decision was its impulsive nature. It was never intended to be a Fourth Amendment case at all, and would not have been were it not for an activist Court.

Dollree Mapp lived on the second floor of a two-family brick house in Cleveland, Ohio, and rented out rooms to boarders. On May 23, 1957, three police officers appeared at her home and demanded entrance, explaining that they were searching for a man in connection with a recent bombing.

After consulting with her attorney on the phone, Ms. Mapp told the officers she wouldn't admit them without a search warrant. Three hours later, the police officers returned, along with others, and forced their way into the house.

Mapp followed behind them, demanding to see the search warrant. Finally, one of the officers produced a piece of paper that Mapp grabbed and shoved down the front of her blouse. A struggle ensued when one of the police officers tried to retrieve the piece of paper. Finally, he handcuffed Mapp and the officers went about their search.

The bombing suspect was not found, and the piece of paper turned out not to be a search warrant. However, the officers did find four books in Ms. Mapp's house: *Affairs of a Troubadour, Little Darlings, London Stage Affairs,* and *Memories of a Hotel Man,* along with a hand-drawn picture later described as being "of a very obscene nature."

Dollree Mapp was convicted of possession of obscene materials, and the appellate courts in Ohio affirmed the decision. She appealed to the U.S. Supreme Court.

The Supreme Court agreed to hear the case because it raised many questions—among them, the constitutionality of the instruction to the jury, the sentence imposed, the statute upon which the conviction was based, and, finally, the conduct of the police. This last issue was limited solely to the police officers' behavior under what was called the "shock the conscience" standard. This standard stemmed from a 1952 case in which police officers pumped a defendant's stomach to retrieve drugs he had swallowed. The Supreme Court held that such behavior "shocks the conscience" and offends the due process clause of the Fourteenth Amendment.

The Fourth Amendment issue—the legality of the police officers' search—was never discussed by the judges in the lower courts. Only the American Civil Liberties Union, in a small point at the end of its brief to the Supreme Court, even suggested that there might be an issue regarding the search of Mapp's residence. The parties never raised the issue at all.

After the oral arguments were heard, the justices held a conference. Still, there was no discussion of the Fourth Amendment or the legality of the search. They did, however, unanimously agree that the Ohio decision violated the First and Fourteenth Amendments. They voted to reverse Mapp's conviction on First Amendment grounds, and Justice Tom Clark was assigned to write the opinion. It appeared that *Mapp* was a fairly basic First Amendment case.

Then some of the justices decided to take an unexpected U-turn, and it changed the course of law for the next thirty-five years and beyond.

When Clark's opinion reached his desk, Justice Potter Stewart was, in his own word, "shocked." It was not the reversal based on the First Amendment that the justices had agreed on. Inexplicably, Clark relied on the Fourth Amendment as the basis for reversal and wrote an opinion that overruled a previous decision on that very issue. The decision was based on arguments that had never even been briefed, argued, or discussed before the Court. If you want to understand the extent of Stewart's amazement and dismay, what Clark and his allies did was comparable to the Supreme Court overruling *Roe* v. *Wade,* the abortion rights decision, with a case involving free speech.

Stewart later speculated that the members of the majority had met in a "rump caucus" to discuss a different basis for the decision. Why would they do this? These were willful men with an agenda and they seized the day, making *Mapp* the case that would showcase the exclusionary rule.

Stewart immediately wrote Clark a note expressing his surprise and questioning the wisdom of overruling an important doctrine in a case in which the issue was not even raised. It seemed to him rash, if not arrogant, to craft a decision of such magnitude without due discussion.

Clark's opinion stood, but the vote of the justices was quite revealing. Although the majority, including Stewart, agreed that Mapp's conviction should be reversed, only four of the judges (a minority) agreed on Fourth Amendment grounds.

Stewart concurred on First Amendment grounds, Black on Fifth Amendment grounds, and three other justices argued that the Fourth Amendment issue was not even properly before the Court.

The end result was that a First Amendment controversy having to do with the right to keep pornography was transformed into the most important search-and-seizure decision in American history.

How does a law that was originally designed to protect us in the privacy of our homes become a barrier to justice? One reason is the way we go about making the law. The U.S. Supreme Court is not like a legislative body that crafts a comprehensive code with specific applications to a wide variety of recurring situations. Rather, the Court merely states a legal philosophy and intent in the deciding of individual cases. The application of Supreme Court decisions to unforeseen circumstances will often be unclear.

Let me give you an example of how a simple issue gets hopelessly tangled. A case is brought before the Supreme Court that deals with an automobile search. Police stop an automobile on the road because it has no tags. They arrest the driver. The issue now is, Can they search the car without a warrant? The Supreme Court has to decide that case, and they decide yes. Although there's a preference for warrants, the Court decides that the automobile search is allowable without a warrant because the car is mobile. In theory, if the police took the time to get a warrant, somebody could drive away with the car. So the Supreme Court creates what is in effect an automobile exception to the warrant requirement. (Incidentally, this isn't the only exception. There are already more than twenty exceptions to the warrant requirement. You can begin to see why the cop on the beat might be confused.)

Now, other cases come along involving automobile searches. In one case, the cops arrest the fellow out on the road and tow his car into the police compound. *They don't search the car; they tow it into the police compound.* After it's in the police compound, they search it.

But wait, now the car is not so mobile. Have the police made a mistake? Does the automobile exception apply once the car is in the police compound? What were the cops supposed to have done? They could have searched the car before they towed it in. But realistically, what's the difference in the violation of privacy if they search it before or after they tow it in?

Let's go beyond that. Let's say the police find a closed suitcase in the trunk of the car. Do they have a right to search it? They can seize the suitcase without searching it, but then it won't be mobile anymore. Does the suitcase in the trunk come under the mobile exception? The answer is: Who knows?

One of the problems with the way law is made is that rules are announced piecemeal as each case arises, but each particular case does not necessarily give us much guidance regarding the multiple types of situations that can arise. Rather, we have to wait for each case to get up to the Supreme Court before we know whether the police acted properly. Furthermore, once a case gets to the Supreme Court, it may be decided by justices who have little or no experience in the criminal justice system, and their rulings are not subject to public or expert scrutiny.

As a judge, I don't have any problem with suppressing evidence if it's been obtained in clear violation of the law. I'm not in favor of cops kicking in doors and ransacking houses without probable or good cause. But that's not the problem with the exclusionary rule. There are certain areas that the police know are off-limits, and if they willfully violate the law, there should be consequences. The problem is that, in more than 90 percent of the cases, the police don't know what the law is. A chief judge riding in the backseat of a police car wouldn't know what the law is!

A police officer often has to act instantaneously and under stressful conditions—not after a careful review of lawyers' briefs and Court decisions. Furthermore, for everything a cop does there are thousands of variations. Every police-citizen encounter, whether it be on the street or in a hallway or in a home or in an automobile or on a bicycle, can develop in any one of a thousand ways. A person can say one thing and a police officer says something else. The person can make one kind of movement, he can make another kind of movement; he has a bulge, he doesn't have a bulge. There are endless scenarios.

The quantum of knowledge is there. Does the cop have reasonable suspicion? Does he have probable cause? It's almost impossible for the law to make an allowance for every single variation. Yet, in effect, that's how we've chosen to do it. We let the Supreme Court decide one automobile case this year and then another automobile case four years later. In the meantime, between year one and year four there have been 3 million automobile searches, and those automobile searches have been conducted by police officers without having any guidance from the first case. So between the first case and the second case you're going to have 3 million decisions going in 3 million different directions.

Simply put, if the Supreme Court could set clear rules for the police to follow, there would be fewer violations. But it is impossible for the Court to establish clear rules that would govern *all* future cases because any clear rules would have *unclear* boundaries. Applying a clear rule to an unforeseen situation can sometimes lead to unjust results.

Because the courts don't know for sure what effects their decisions will have on police, and because overturning a conviction has high social costs, the courts strain the precedents to preserve convictions. This straining produces precedents that uphold police activity at the outer margin of permissibility. Decisions may ultimately be result-oriented and poorly reasoned.

The automobile exception has been the premier example of Supreme Court confusion. The Court itself has called our law on the automobile exception "intolerably confusing."

I do not question the need for effective remedies to give meaning to the protections of the Fourth Amendment. Without remedies, there are no rights. But the hope that the exclusionary rule would be that "effective remedy" has never been realized.

Much of the argument about search and seizure rests on one question: What constitutes reasonable suspicion on the part of the police? We wrestled with that issue in my New York City courtroom in the case of Darrell Nickelson.

These are the facts of the case: On October 5, 1993, Sergeant Thomas J. Keane and Police Officers John Dalessio and William Aragundi, members of an anticrime unit assigned to the 32nd Precinct, were patrolling in plainclothes in an unmarked car. It was 4:00 in the afternoon.

While they were stopped at a red light at Seventh Avenue and 127th Street, the officers became aware of a black Buick with a livery license plate directly in front of their vehicle. They noticed that the passenger wore a fishing cap pulled low over his face, and he repeatedly, and nervously, looked from left to right. When the light changed, the livery cab proceeded south on Seventh Avenue and signaled to make a left turn onto 124th Street. While the Buick waited to make the turn, the passenger looked back in the direction of the officers, making eye contact with them for a few seconds. He turned away, then looked back and made eye contact with the officers a second time. The officers were suspicious. During the past ten months, there had been some forty cab robberies in the 32nd Precinct, most involving livery cabs. The passenger's movements and glances gave them reason to suspect that something—perhaps a robbery—might be about to happen. The police officers followed the Buick as it made the turn. When the passenger looked back at them a third time,

Sergeant Keane decided to stop the livery cab to make sure the driver was okay. He placed his bubble light on the dashboard, turned on his siren and headlights, and stopped the Buick. Immediately, the passenger tried to jump out of the car, but he was stopped by Officers Aragundi and Dalessio. When they looked inside, they found a fully loaded nine-millimeter automatic stuffed in a magazine pouch that was hanging from behind the driver's seat, directly in front of where the passenger was sitting. They arrested the passenger, Darrell Nickelson, and charged him with illegal possession of a weapon. It turned out that Nickelson was a persistent violent felon, and his possession of a loaded weapon was not only illegal but a pretty clear indication that he was headed for more trouble.

Nickelson's attorney made a motion to suppress the gun on the grounds that there was no cause for police to stop the vehicle. It had not violated any traffic regulations. Furthermore, case law had established that furtive gestures by a vehicle's occupant, absent other factors, do not in themselves suggest criminal activity.

At the hearing on the motion to suppress, Sergeant Keane testified that, given the recent spate of livery cab robberies, he had found Nickelson's gestures suspicious.

In forming my opinion, I struggled over two conflicting factors. The first was the common sense of the situation. Sergeant Keane was an experienced police officer with more than ten years on the force. He could be trusted to make a judgment call about suspicious behavior. Furthermore, the incident occurred in a high-crime area where many cab robberies had occurred in recent months.

On the other hand, a police officer may not infer criminal behavior based solely on a person's furtive actions—without supportive information. For example, if the driver had flashed his high beams signaling trouble, or otherwise indicated distress, that would have been different.

I had no choice under current New York law but to suppress the weapon, but it galled me. This was, in my opinion, a frustrating example of the law's arbitrariness and ambiguity. By ruling in favor of the defendant, as I was forced by law to do, I was saying to police officers that their judgment and experience would be given little weight in the court of law. They might as well shut off their five senses and ignore what is taking place around them.

We want the government to act *effectively* but in a *restrained* way. We want to be protected both in our exercise of liberty and in the event the law turns against us. If our son is stopped for driving recklessly on the country's roads, we want to be sure that he's treated fairly.

But you can't count on it, because the system makes it a lottery. And sometimes the results will just break your heart. The case of *Coolidge* v. *New Hampshire* was a shocking example. But no less so than the case of Angela Skinner, another astounding example of human suffering dismissed and justice denied on a technicality.

Detroit police officers John Collins and Phillip Ratliff responded to a call that Angela Skinner, a fourteen-year-old girl, was missing and was suspected of being held against her will in the apartment of one Lee Erwin Johnson. Collins and Ratliff went to the apartment and knocked on the door. It was opened by Angela Skinner, but she was separated from police by a padlocked armored gate. With the help of a neighbor's tools, the officers cut the padlock and entered the apartment. Johnson wasn't home.

Angela told Collins and Ratliff that she had been held in the apartment for four days. Johnson had repeatedly raped her and threatened to shoot her or her family if she tried to escape. She told the officers that Johnson threatened her with guns, and she pointed to a closet where the guns were kept. Collins and Ratliff seized three guns and ammunition from the closet. A full search of the apartment was not conducted at that time.

Johnson had a long criminal record, including four prior arrests for violent felonies. He was found by a trial court to be a career criminal, and was sentenced to fifteen years in jail. The trial court refused to suppress the weapons seized, concluding that seizure was justified by the circumstances and by Skinner's consent.

The court of appeals, however, reversed the decision in what can only be described as a bizarre twist. The court stated that the presence of an armored door showed that Skinner clearly did not have authority to allow the officers to enter the apartment! Nor did she have authority to direct them to the closet where the guns were stored. The court felt that once the police officers had freed Skinner, they had ample time to get a search warrant.

This absurd decision completely ignores the facts of the case. More reasoned minds might suggest that Johnson forfeited his right to privacy when he kidnapped and locked Angela Skinner in his apartment.

Even though the police were found to have a justifiable reason to enter the apartment without a search warrant, the court found they did not have the right to open the closet. By law, searches are limited to specific areas, and this is understandable. The police can't just randomly invade a house and turn everything upside down. They must be disciplined in their approach. They must have an idea of what they're searching for.

Now, generally, you can particularize. You can say your probable cause may be that a person was seen going into the apartment with a gun and stolen property. So you would say that the stolen property consists of a lamp and a teapot and a gun, and that's the property you want to recover. In effect, the item to be searched for defines and limits the area that may be searched. For example, you can't search for a lamp in a drawer because a lamp doesn't fit in a drawer. However, if you go in looking for a stolen watch, obviously you can look in that drawer. If you find three pounds of heroin in the drawer, you can seize it because it was in plain view.

In the case of Angela Skinner, the police did not have permission from the defendant to look for guns in the closet. Since the police did not have a search warrant and the guns were not in "plain view," the weapons were suppressed.

Does this make any sense? Why is the law so sensitive about protecting the privacy of a man who was proven to have locked a child in an apartment for four days? Because that is the law. The insane logic of it would have given Thomas Aquinas a headache.

There was one dissenter in the decision, Judge Richard F. Suhrheinrich. In what seems to me to be the lone voice of reason, he wrote: "I would hold that when the defendant converted his apartment from a home to a prison, he forfeited whatever reasonable expectation of privacy he had. Here . . . the defendant converted his home into the very instrumentality of his crime . . . once the police broke into the defendant's makeshift jail and freed his captive they were free to seize any means he had employed to hold her against her will."

To be sure, the police officers could have secured the apartment and obtained a search warrant—although, since the defendant was not present, the warrant could not have been served upon him. And securing the apartment would have required more police officers and a delay in seizing loaded weapons.

Which seems more *reasonable* to you? The policemen's action or the court's action?

A knowledgeable New York judge, Frank Weissberg, has said to me in despair, "The law on search and seizure is so unpredictable that if my only concern was being affirmed by an appellate court, without regard to the merits of the case, I don't think I could be sure of that result more than sixty percent of the time."

Sadly, I have found the same thing to be true. Although the area of search and seizure has been my major specialization for many years, I can't predict what the courts are going to do. It seems that every time they act to make the law clearer, they only succeed in making it foggier—as if they were trying to wash windows with muddy water.

———

Back in 1980, a good friend of mine, Nick Scoppetta, was the director of the Institute of Judicial Administration at New York University Law School. Every summer, the institute invites appellate judges from all over the country to attend a monthlong series of lectures and workshops. Nick asked me if I would give the judges a refresher course on recent developments in the law of search and seizure. I agreed. And as luck would have it, the U.S. Supreme Court issued its final round of decisions the last week of June, and there were two cases that stood out quite starkly as examples of the impenetrable nature of search-and-seizure laws. When the rulings were announced, the appellate judges were in transit to New York and didn't have a chance to read the two decisions.

I had read them, however, and I couldn't have anticipated the logic or the results. I decided to present the facts of these two cases to the appellate judges and see how they—without prior knowledge, just using their understanding of the law and their powers of reasoning—would decide the cases. It seemed like a legitimate test.

Here are the facts as they appeared in the Supreme Court decisions and as I presented them to the appellate judges:

Case One involved a group of pornographers in St. Petersburg, Florida, who sent a package of pornographic films to Atlanta, Georgia—to the attention of a certain female secretary. Because of her physical attributes, this secretary was referred to as "Legs."

The pornographers packed 871 videocassettes into twelve large, securely sealed boxes and sent the boxes in care of "Legs, Inc." to Atlanta. They used a false return address.

The shipment was mistakenly delivered by a private carrier to a substation in the suburbs of Atlanta where "L'Eggs Products, Inc.," an egg candling factory, regularly received deliveries. (Egg candling is a process whereby eggs are held up to the light to determine if they are good eggs.) The employees of the egg candling factory opened the boxes and found the cassettes. They didn't have to use their imagination to figure out the contents of these cassettes. Each box had a little cover. On one side was a written description of the contents, and on the other side was a graphic picture of what was inside.

The L'Eggs employees immediately realized that these were not eggs, and they called the FBI. The FBI responded, and the L'Eggs employees handed over the boxes of pornographic videos. The FBI agents returned to their office, where they viewed the films and determined that they were pornographic. They ultimately arrested the pornographers. At the trial, the judge denied a defense motion to suppress the tapes. He ruled that the ficticious name of both shipper and addressee amounted to a relinquishment of any reasonable expectation of privacy. That was Case One.

Next, I described to my captive audience of appellate judges the facts of Case Two, which involved an Internal Revenue Service investigation called Operation Trade Winds. Investigators had come to believe that many Americans were avoiding their taxes by opening offshore bank accounts in the Bahama Islands. So they devised a scheme that they knew was unlawful. As a matter of fact, the Supreme Court later referred to it as "bad-faith hostility" against the Fourth Amendment.

This was the scheme: The IRS hired a private investigator who hired a prostitute who lured a Bahamian banker to Florida. When he arrived in Florida with his attaché case filled with Bahamian bank records, the prostitute said, "Let's go out for dinner, and then I'll show you a good time." He was completely distracted by her charm and he agreed. They went out to dinner, at which time IRS agents entered the banker's hotel room, broke into his attaché case, photographed all of the Bahamian bank records, closed the attaché case, and left the apartment.

Using the Bahamian bank records as a guide, the IRS agents called the people who had bank accounts in the Bahamas before a grand jury. When the suspects denied they had bank accounts in the Bahamas, they were indicted for perjury. The IRS was able to show they were lying because they had possession of the bank records. One of the defendants decided this was an unlawful invasion of privacy, and he appealed.

These were the two cases the Supreme Court ruled on. In the first, there was a move to suppress the pornographic movies; in the other, a man who had been indicted for perjury argued that the FBI had no right to his bank records.

I asked the fifty appellate judges in the room: "Based on your experience, from all parts of the country, how would you decide those cases if they came to you?"

The judges overwhelmingly replied that they would suppress the evidence taken from the Bahamian banker because the IRS acted with bad-faith hostility to Fourth Amendment values. And they would deny the motion to suppress the pornographic films because the FBI acted properly. They didn't even seize anything; the boxes were handed to them. It would have been a dereliction of duty for them not to have gone and picked up the boxes.

The Supreme Court's decisions were exactly the opposite: The pornography was suppressed and the Bahamian records were allowed.

Why were the pornographic tapes suppressed? The Court determined that the FBI's failure to get a search warrant invalidated their search. But wait a minute. What were they "searching" for? If they got a warrant to search, who were they going to serve it on? The people who sent the movies had used false names and a fictitious address, so a warrant couldn't be served on them. Nevertheless, the Supreme Court determined that there should have been a search warrant obtained before the tapes were viewed by the FBI. The decision wasn't unanimous. The Court ruled five to four, and there were four separate opinions. The confusion of the Court was visited upon the masses.

Let's look at Case Two. The IRS behaved badly. They hired prostitutes for burglaries. The Court even said the actions of the IRS agents were illegal. You'd think there would be plenty of reason to suppress the bank records, since the man who appealed was indicted for perjury based on illegally seized records. But the Court determined that this man's privacy was not violated because it wasn't his attaché case that was invaded; it was the Bahamian banker's attaché case that was invaded. So no interest of his personal privacy was lost, and he had no standing to protest.

If you're baffled by these results, you're in good company. Fifty appellate judges from across the nation join you in your confusion. The law is unknowable. In his dissent, Justice Harry Blackmun made the point: "We tend occasionally to strain credulity and to spin the thread of argument so thin that we depart from . . . common sense."

I struggle with these issues every day. When we're arguing the law in the heady atmosphere of conferences and universities, it's easy to forget that we are talking about real people, real crimes, real human suffering. We are also talking about repeatedly compromising the integrity of the law by making it arbitrary and unknowable.

Much of the time, the deliverance of justice comes down to the cop on the beat. And every day of the week, cops have to make quick decisions under highly stressful circumstances, burdened by the fogginess of the law.

Some years back, a case came before me that seemed sadly typical. Police Officer Colleran was in his radio patrol car, driving through the late-night streets of New York City. Shortly before midnight, his radio squawked out a 911 call: A black man, armed with a gun, was seen entering a red-brick building at 115th Street and Fifth Avenue. The man was described as walking with a limp and wearing a jacket and red sneakers.

How should Officer Colleran have proceeded? Presumably, we the citizenry expect him to go investigate the call and try to check out the man with the gun. And that's what he did. He drove to the scene within a minute and spotted a black man with red sneakers, walking with a limp, exiting a bar across the street from the given location.

Now, what action should Colleran take? Well, we know that if he got out of the car and immediately started clubbing the black man over the head it would be a grievous violation of the man's rights. He didn't do that. Instead, he got out of his car, drew his own gun, and shouted, "Police officer. Stop!" The man stopped and Officer Colleran patted him down, felt the gun, recovered it, and made an arrest. Could there be a simpler case in the world?

It seems to me the police officer acted reasonably. He did what he was supposed to do, what the people expect a police officer to do. When the case came before me, the defense lawyer argued that the gun should be suppressed because Colleran's action was based on an anonymous tip. I denied the motion. The defendant was convicted of attempted possession of a weapon and sentenced as a second-felony offender to one and a half to three years.

The case went up to the appellate division. The appellate division reversed me three to two. Why? Because Officer Colleran didn't know the source of the 911 call. So, according to the court, he didn't know what information that person had when he said the man had the gun. It was an anonymous informant.

According to the appellate division, Colleran should have ignored the call since he didn't know its source or reliability. The court felt the officer was acting too harshly by jumping out of his car and pulling a gun. They even suggested that he should have strolled up to the limping man with the red sneakers, without drawing his gun, and said words to the effect of, "Pardon me, sir. We received a report that you may have a gun and I'm just inquiring about that." At which point the man, if he had even the vaguest inkling of his rights, might well reply, "I appreciate your interest, Officer, but I'm fine. I'll see you around." And that would be the end of it. The message to the cop on the beat is, "The next time you get a radio call of a man with a gun, don't investigate, take a break."

Does this scenario reflect the intention of the Constitution? The laws of society are essentially a contract with the people that says, "You will not take the law into your own hands; we will appoint officers of the law to protect you." But what has happened is that the contract is being broken every day. And when citizens see obviously guilty and perhaps dangerous criminals being allowed to go free, there is a temptation to take the law into their own hands.

If you suppress evidence, you're suppressing truth. It is my belief that the benefits of the exclusionary rule in protecting the privacy of the citizen are greatly outweighed by its burden on the truth-seeking process and by reduced crime control. Remember, there is never any question of the reliability of the evidence. We rightly exclude evidence when it is not reliable. However, the method of search does not reduce the reliability of the evidence.

The main argument adopted by the Supreme Court in *Mapp* was that the exclusionary rule is necessary because nothing else works. But even if it is true that nothing *else* works, that does not guarantee that the exclusionary rule works. This logic reminds me of the old joke about the drunk who is found look-ing for his keys under a lamppost. When questioned, he explains that he lost the keys some blocks away. "But I didn't look there," he says, "because it was too dark."

Is there a satisfactory resolution to this conundrum? Is there a better way? Let's examine it.

First, we should ask the obvious and most relevant ques-tion: Is the exclusionary rule an effective deterrent to police misbehavior? As the Supreme Court itself has noted, "Rejec-tion of evidence does nothing to punish the wrong-doing offi-cial, while it may, and likely will, release the wrong-doing defendant."

Consider this:

- With rare exceptions, police departments do not sanction police officers or hold them responsible when evidence is excluded. They may not even know about it.
- The sanction of suppression is visited on the prosecutor, whose case is then weakened or destroyed. The DA has no control over the police department.
- Even if police officers try to take the exclusionary rule to heart, its impact is reduced by the practical realities of law enforcement. Police officers do not have the time, inclina-tion, or training to read and understand the nuances of appellate decisions that define standards of conduct. The impact of these decisions on police officers is also reduced by the lengthy time lapse—often years—between the origi-nal police action and its final judicial evaluation.

- Most important, the legal doctrines the exclusionary rule enforces are so complicated and tangled that the police (and even judges themselves) cannot determine in advance what a majority of the Supreme Court will find. If the police do not understand the rules, how can they enforce them?

Say what you will about justice, the hallmarks of the exclusionary rule are irrationality, arbitrariness, and a lack of proportion. Whenever it is applied, a criminal goes free—no matter how serious the crime or minor the police intrusion. The bald fact is that it is more lottery than law.

There is a patchwork quality to the law, precisely because it does not follow a historical straight line. Rather, like Topsy, it just "growed," and the outcome is not always practical or fair.

The remedy to this disarray is so simple that it has escaped us for decades.

The greatest criticism of the exclusionary rule is that it is mandatory. Imagine for a moment that the exclusionary rule was discretionary instead of mandatory. This model uses *reasonableness* as a guide, and proposes that we not try to set detailed guidelines for police behavior in every possible situation. In its place the court will determine whether the search and seizure is reasonable by considering all relevant factors on a case-by-case basis. For example:

- Was there probable cause?
- Was a search warrant obtained?

- Were there exigent circumstances that made obtaining a search warrant unfeasible?
- What was the nature of the intrusion?
- What was the quantum of evidence?
- What was the seriousness of the crime under investigation?
- Was the defendant believed to be dangerous?

And so on. Logic, the standard of reasonableness, prevails. This model is roughly the current practice in Germany, where it works well. The important consideration in the German system is whether the intrusion on a defendant's privacy is proportional to the seriousness of the offense. This is applied on a case-by-case basis.

In most cases, the standard of reasonableness reflects the result, though not the reasoning, of current Supreme Court cases. The Supreme Court has often referred to reasonableness as the "fundamental inquiry" in Fourth Amendment issues.

As Professor Craig Bradley of the Indiana University School of Law, an expert on the subject, has pointed out, requiring police officers to use their common sense, and judging them by that standard, seems more likely to produce sensible results than does a set of unknowable rules and vague exceptions that neither the police nor the courts can understand.

And, oh, what a remarkable thing it would be if justice were applied with such a simple eye to common sense!

| 3 |

THE SILENCE OF THE FOX

Miranda and the Quagmire of Coercion,
Confession, and Conscience

> Peaceful interrogation is not one of the dark
> moments of the law.
>
> JOHN MARSHALL HARLAN,
> U.S. Supreme Court,
> *Miranda* dissent, 1966

"Officer, I killed a woman."

Denver police officer Patrick Anderson, on traffic duty, frowned skeptically at the distraught man standing before him.

"You what?"

The man's eyes darted nervously. "My name is Francis Connelly," he said. "I murdered someone and I want to confess. I'll tell you . . ."

Instinctively, Anderson held up a hand to stop the rush of words. "Sir, wait a minute. Before you say anything, I must advise you of your rights." He proceeded to state the *Miranda* warning.

Connelly shook his head impatiently. "Yeah, I know all that. I don't care. I want to talk."

Anderson considered the man uneasily. "Have you been drinking, sir?" he asked.

"No."

"Are you under the influence of drugs?"

"No."

"I must warn you again before you say anything that you have the right to remain silent . . ."

"It's all right," Connelly interrupted. "My conscience is bothering me. I want to confess."

Anderson was baffled. Nothing like this had ever happened to him before. He told Connelly to wait a minute and he radioed his superior. "I have a man here who says he wants to confess to a murder. What should I do?"

Anderson was instructed to wait with Connelly and say nothing. Soon after, Steven Antuna, a homicide detective, arrived on the scene. He once again advised Connelly of his rights, then asked, "So, what's on your mind?"

"I came to Denver from Boston," Connelly said. "I killed a girl here last year, sometime during November 1982. Her name was Mary Ann Junta. I want to confess."

The officers took Connelly to the police station, and a search of police records revealed that the body of an unidentified female had been found in April 1983. Connelly readily agreed to take Detective Antuna and Sergeant Thomas Haney to the scene of the killing. They got in a car and, following Connelly's directions, proceeded to the location of the crime. Connelly pointed out the exact spot where he said the murder had occurred. His recollection seemed to be clear and sane. At no time did the detectives get any indication that he was suffering from mental illness. He merely seemed to be a man with a guilty conscience.

Connelly was held overnight. On the following morning, during an interview with the public defender's office, he became visibly disoriented and began giving confused answers. For the first time, he stated that "voices" had told him to go to Denver and "confess."

Connelly was sent to a hospital for an evaluation to determine if he was mentally competent to assist in his own defense. Doctors there found him competent, and it was decided to proceed to trial. But at a pretrial hearing Connelly's lawyer moved to suppress Connelly's statements to the police. A psychiatrist testified that Connelly was psychotic the day he confessed. He had been following "the voice of God," which had directed him to fly from Boston to Denver and confess to the killing. Following these "command hallucinations," he approached Police Officer Anderson and confessed.

The psychiatrist testified that Connelly's condition interfered with his volitional abilities and his ability to make free and rational choices. It did not, however, interfere with Connelly's cognitive abilities, so he understood his rights when the police officers advised him that he need not speak.

The doctor admitted that the voices could be Connelly's interpretation of his own guilt, but felt that it was the defendant's psychosis that motivated his confession. The Colorado trial court suppressed Connelly's confession because it was "involuntary"—not a product of his rational intellect and free will. Admittedly, the police officers had done nothing wrong. There was no coercion. Indeed, they used abundant care to make sure Connelly understood his rights.

The U.S. Supreme Court overruled Colorado's decision to suppress Connelly's statements, since there was no action by the police officers that compelled him to confess. The Court noted that there is no right of a defendant to confess only when he is "totally rational and properly motivated."

The primary concern of the Court in applying *Miranda* is to protect defendants against police abuse, to assure that confessions are voluntary. But as Connelly's case demonstrated, the concept of voluntariness is a slippery one.

We all have images branded on our minds from movies, books, and the true tales of human civilization. These are images of brutal force, of torture, of governments using excessive means to pry confessions out of the innocent as well as the guilty.

But we're equally familiar with the positive use of government power to apprehend criminals. Throughout history, governments have acted to protect their citizens by seeking out people suspected of wrongdoing, and asking them questions about their conduct. It's common sense that the most reasonable and effective way to get information is to ask someone about it.

Interrogation of suspects was always a primary method of law enforcement, and we considered it a proper prerogative of authority. And if, in the midst of questioning, the defendant confessed, then bravo! In one respect he had begun his return to civilized society by admitting his wrongdoing, by telling the truth.

Society, however, has long known that interrogation might be accompanied by the unlawful use of force. So we've been concerned about regulating interrogation so that it's a test of veracity, not of endurance. There is a historic tension between the government's need to protect its citizens and its concern that this be done in a decent manner.

In the United States, until recently, incommunicado detention and questioning of suspects who were lawfully arrested was a common part of the investigative process. The police exercised this authority largely without supervision; such broad discretion was believed to be "indispensable to crime detection." Consistent with this practice, a confession was believed to be a reliable form of evidence and its truth could often be verified—for instance, if a murder weapon was found where the defendant said it was.

As late as the early 1960s, the Supreme Court did not feel compelled to burden the government with any special duty to inform the suspect that he didn't have to talk. The Court was not troubled by the fear that defendants would wrongly believe that they were obliged to answer police questions. Everyone understood that the government's job was not to counsel a defendant but to question him. Indeed, some pressuring of a defendant was considered absolutely permissible; how else would you get him to confess?

Professor Gerald M. Caplan, in his article "Questioning *Miranda*" (*Vanderbilt Law Review*, Nov. 1985), writes that during the time these views prevailed, there was greater public confidence in police, and confessions were perceived as expressions of remorse, not force. Today, there is less interest in reconciling the rights of a suspect with effective interrogation. Indeed, to many, these are irreconcilable goals. Confession is seen as the product of coercion, trickery, or deceit.

There is also a different attitude toward suspects. Many argue that the police should treat those who are justifiably suspected of committing a crime no differently than non-suspects. Others would prohibit police questioning entirely, without regard for the impact on public safety. Furthermore, the suspect who makes a confession is viewed as in some way handicapped—a member of a minority group or a person under great stress of whom the police have taken advantage.

Miranda has become an integral part of the process of criminal justice. But as with most of our judicial formalities, the route to *Miranda* was long and circuitous, involving many side trips. On its journey it gathered a certain momentum beyond necessity, so that by the time the law was finally formulated, it was muddied by the grime of ill-conceived policy.

I think the place *Miranda* really started was back in 1936 with a case called *Brown* v. *Mississippi*. The "third degree"—often amounting to a twentieth-century version of the rack—was pervasive in the United States then, especially in the South. A sheriff beat up Brown with a metal-buckled leather strap. The U.S. Supreme Court, under the due process clause of the Fourteenth Amendment, reversed the conviction, saying this was a trial by ordeal, not a fair trial. Certainly, we all agree that in a civilized society, police officers should not be free to torture people they have in custody.

But what if the coercion is less violent? That question came up for decision in *Chambers* v. *Florida* in 1940, where the Court sought to define due process in less violent situations. Chambers was threatened by mob violence and questioned by four police officers continuously for five days and an entire night before his "sunrise confession."

The Supreme Court reversed the conviction, finding that the confession was unreliable because it was not necessarily the product of Chambers's own perception of events. In essence, the confession was not "voluntary."

Other cases followed on the heels of *Brown* and *Chambers,* establishing a body of law in which one can identify the difficulties of regulating police conduct. At issue was the definition of coercion and the interest in being fair to a suspect in custody. Restrictions on police questioning grew out of these rulings.

Once these restrictions were set in place by the Supreme Court, future cases simply added weight to the same faulty premises—establishing, for example, that the "voluntary" confession must be obtained fairly, as if this were a sporting contest rather than a search for truth. More and more, the issue was not whether the confession was true but whether there was any suspect conduct on the part of police to procure it. A conviction would be reversed if the Court found that the method of interrogation was so unfair that the defendant's free will was overborne. It was clear that if the police engaged in certain practices—prolonged detention, relay questioning, threats, intimidation, physical force, promises of benefit, denial of food or sleep—they did so at their own peril.

The problem with this approach, says Professor Caplan, was that "its elusive boundaries made the admissibility of a confession difficult to predict." Police interrogators were walking on eggshells to make sure the confession was voluntary and fairly obtained. Still, by the 1960s, the police were operating with far greater sensitivity to constitutional requirements. After nearly thirty years of judicial development, the voluntariness test was an evolving moral inquiry into what was decent and fair in police interrogation practices.

Then, in 1962, came the case of *Gallegos* v. *Colorado*—what might be considered an ideological forerunner to *Miranda*.

Gallegos, a "child of fourteen," and two friends followed an elderly man into his hotel and used a ruse to enter his room. They then assaulted him and stole $13; it was their second assault that day and this time the victim died. Later, a juvenile officer spotted Gallegos sitting on a curb with his two younger brothers. Since they matched the description of the felons, the officer identified himself and invited the boys to sit in his car. Gallegos entered the car and almost immediately admitted to the assault and robbery. He repeated his confession the next day, and five days later he signed a confession.

Gallegos was not intensely questioned, nor was he mis-treated in any way. Before he made and signed the confession he was advised of his right to counsel, his right to remain silent, and his right to have his family present. He signed the confession, stating that he did not want an attorney.

Gallegos was sentenced to life in prison.

In terms of the traditional criteria of voluntariness, there was little to recommend reversal. However, when the Court reviewed the case, weight was given to Gallegos's youth and the failure of police officers to grant his parents immediate access to him. In addition, the Court focused on the superior status of the police: "We deal with a person [the defendant] who is not equal to the police in knowledge and under-standing."

The assertion that Gallegos was "not equal to the police," while correct, was jarring. Why should this be relevant to whether an otherwise voluntary confession is admissible as evidence?

Professor Caplan notes that prior to *Gallegos,* the Supreme Court had never conceptualized the problems of interroga-tion in terms of equality. It's like saying, "The defendant was no match for the cops! They were smarter, craftier, better armed, and better educated. It wasn't fair to the defendant, so we should let him go."

But wait a minute. Do we *want* it to be an equal contest? Do we want criminals to be as smart or smarter than the cops?

The absurdity continued two years later with the case of *Escobedo* v. *Illinois.* After the shooting of his brother-in-law, Danny Escobedo was questioned for several hours about the killing before his attorney secured his release. He made no statement during this period. Ten days later, the police learned from another suspect, a man named DiGerlando, that Escobedo had been the triggerman. Escobedo was again arrested and questioned. During this second interrogation, Escobedo asked to see his attorney, while at the same time his attorney was outside unsuccessfully trying to see him.

Meanwhile, in the interrogation room, Escobedo was calling DiGerlando a liar. One of the detectives challenged him, "Will you say it to his face?" Escobedo agreed. DiGerlando was brought in and Escobedo cried, "I didn't shoot Manuel, you did it!" With those words, he implicated himself in the murder by stating firsthand knowledge of the killing.

On its facts, Escobedo's case bore little resemblance to prior cases. The police had used no force, no intimidation, no relay questioning, no denials of food and sleep. Further, Escobedo had no special handicap. He was not mentally disturbed, illiterate, a victim of discrimination, or inexperienced in the ways of the criminal justice system. Most important, he had retained an attorney, and in prior discussions his attorney had advised him what to do in the event of police interrogation.

Even so, the Court reversed Escobedo's conviction in a five-four decision based solely on the fact that his attorney was not in the room at the moment he made the incriminating statement. The Court decided Escobedo's case on the basis of the Sixth Amendment right to counsel, not the Fifth Amendment.

Escobedo triggered great interest in police investigative practices. After *Escobedo,* the American Bar Association, the

American Law Institute, and the National Crime Commission all independently undertook studies of police methods. In addition, the law enforcement establishment engaged in some critical self-examination. The results of these studies clearly showed that the police were more restrained and law abiding than ever. Given that, there was no reason for the Court to act hastily to place even more restrictions on the police. But that's exactly what it was prepared to do.

Miranda was the case that put the seal on several decades of Court decisions. In my judgment, it was folly—a terrible decision atop many other terrible decisions.

Miranda was really four cases consolidated for decision. The name attached to the case was that of Ernesto Miranda, arrested for and convicted of rape.

Ernesto Miranda almost escaped detection. His teenage victim was shy and easily confused, and there were apparent discrepancies in her initial report to the police. When Miranda was placed in a lineup with only two others, she could not make a positive identification.

But the investigating police, convinced that the young girl was truthful, employed a routine trick to encourage Miranda to confess. Following the lineup, Miranda asked, "How'd I do?" The police answered, "You flunked."

Miranda's questioning was mild. It was conducted midday by two police officers and it lasted only two hours. Before it was over, he had confessed not only to the rape for which he had been arrested, but also to the attempted rape of a second person and trying to rob a third. Once Miranda had signed a confession, the police brought the victim into the interrogation room and asked if he recognized her. "That's the girl," he replied.

When Miranda made the identification, he still believed the girl had picked him out of the lineup. However, neither this deception nor anything else about the way Miranda was questioned bothered the Supreme Court. Three years after Miranda committed the rape, the U.S. Supreme Court had another concern weighing on its mind. And it was to appease this concern that the decision in *Miranda* was manipulated.

The Court was interested in creating an objective standard that would free courts from the task of determining whether a defendant was actually coerced into making a confession. On the face of it, it seems ridiculous that a rigid standard could be used to address such an individual issue. But this is precisely what the Court sought to do.

Using the Fifth Amendment standard against compulsion as a rationale, the Court declared that, prior to questioning, the police must warn a suspect in custody that he has the right to remain silent, any statements he makes might be used against him, and he has the right to the presence of counsel, retained or appointed.

The warning was to be given in every case of custodial interrogation. If the police failed to give the warning, any statement, however voluntary, would be treated as coerced and therefore suppressed. And while a suspect could waive his rights, a heavy burden was on the government to show that he had knowingly and intelligently done so. *Miranda* created a high Fifth Amendment hurdle at the threshold of every police inquiry. Some years after *Miranda,* Justices Brennan and Marshall even wrote that "the cost" of *Miranda* is that "some voluntary statements will be excluded."

It was custodial interrogation itself—apart from its duration or intensity or the tactics employed—that was of concern. If a suspect volunteered a statement, it would be admissible. However, once a question was asked, any response would be barred unless the *Miranda* warning was given and a waiver obtained.

Professor Caplan suggests that in *Miranda,* the Court established a different view of an arrested person. Previously, Supreme Court decisions saw the arrestee "as a hardy suspect—unwilling to confess and able to resist police questioning for hours without having his will overborne." With *Miranda,* it saw the very fact of custodial questioning as a grave threat to free will.

No one knows whether it was the Court's intention to eliminate all or nearly all custodial interrogation, or whether the majority of five shared a common intention. But it appears that the Court expected the presence of counsel at the police station to be routine—something that never came to be—and its waiver extraordinary. It was significant that only after the *Miranda* opinion had taken up more than fifty pages did it then turn to the facts of the four cases before the Court. Courts are not supposed to belabor issues and opinions that are not central to the decision. Their role is to decide cases, not give advice. But *Miranda* went into issues of impeachment and waiver and the effect of silence. It was an unprecedented decision in its broad form, and it left a maelstrom of unanswered questions.

Was it now wrong for the police to urge a person to confess, or for counsel to allow or advise his client to do so? Professor Caplan says that Justice Earl Warren's opinion for the Supreme Court "treats a confession as an act of poor judgment by a vulnerable person outmaneuvered by the police."

As Justice Thurgood Marshall put it in a statement clearly relevant to the *Miranda* argument, "No sane person would knowingly relinquish a right to be free of compulsion."

So, the idealistic impulse toward protecting individuals from overbearing state authority has resulted in a system where we deny people the opportunity to take responsibility for their criminal acts. In our system, a man or woman who takes responsibility must be crazy!

And what's the responsibility of the police? Is it really the police officer's job to serve as a counselor to an arrested person? In my mind, requiring a police officer to tell a murder or rape suspect that he need not answer questions seems altogether too charitable. It suggests an ambivalence toward the suspect and his deed. Does not the *Miranda* warning encourage the defendant to withhold information?

Why is such generosity called for? Once again, we've thrown the baby out with the bathwater. It's a far cry from coercing confessions to saying, in effect, "I *urge* you not to confess."

Miranda has been called, derisively, a "fox hunter's argument"—that is, the defendant, like a fox during a hunt, must be given a fair chance to escape. In this way, the criminal justice system becomes a sporting event in which the defendant has a sporting chance to evade society's punishment.

To a rational person, even a compassionate person, this is nonsense.

I agree that intelligent people do sometimes object to police interrogation because they claim the suspect is no match for the police. But why would we try to advocate equality between a defendant and a police officer—unless we thought the system was a game, a sport, a fox hunt?

A desire for equality cannot be a justification for restrictions on police interrogation. And we might reasonably wonder why a rational person should worry that a guilty suspect's chances of acquittal have been reduced. Without successful pretrial investigation, the case would never come to trial.

Professor Yale Kamisar, a well-known and highly respected liberal professor at the University of Michigan Law School, wrote a piece some years ago in which he said he found it incomprehensible that the Constitution could require so much protection for the defendant in the "mansion" of the courtroom and so little in the "gatehouse" of the police station.

I don't believe the "gatehouse" stomps on rights. But even if I did believe it, we must understand that the purpose of the police station is far different from the purpose of the courtroom. It should be obvious that interrogation and trial have disparate goals.

As Professor Joseph D. Grano, a legal scholar, has pointed out, a trial, in an adversary system, enables each party to present its case to a disinterested fact finder who does not have independent fact-gathering authority. So, equality between the parties in a courtroom furthers the interest in accurate fact finding. But if we assume (as we should) that the law will not permit interrogation techniques that create an undue risk of false confession, then equality in the police station thwarts rather than serves the goal of truth. By definition and design, police interrogation involves one party trying to learn the truth from another party who is not inclined to reveal it.

Sometimes (bizarrely, I think), the fox hunt argument is modified to express egalitarian notions: If sophisticated persons have the means to escape, so, too, should the less sophisticated. But why should inequality among suspects at the investigative stage be of concern? Indeed, it should be a source of regret that some guilty suspects are resourceful enough to evade detection and conviction. What purpose is served in the equal acquittal of the guilty?

The sporting theory of justice is not the only argument against police interrogation. The other is that the Fifth Amendment rests on the premise that ours is an accusatorial rather than an inquisitorial system of justice. That's true in a trial—for what is a trial but an accusatory event?

Police investigation, however, is basically inquisitorial, whether we want to call it that or not. What other purpose is there? A police investigation involves prying, pursuing, and trying to discover that which is unknown. We permit this when we require a defendant to stand in a lineup, when we take samples of his blood for testing, when we ask for handwriting samples, when we fingerprint him.

It seems that we are forever ambivalent about the scope of our law enforcement procedures. We want criminals apprehended. We're delighted when they confess. But then we ignore their guilt and the grievousness of their crime while we worry ourselves to death about whether the police asked questions.

Maybe our confusion has to do with the meaning of respect and human dignity. The Fifth Amendment embodies the moral belief that government must respect the rights of all individuals. Is straightforward questioning in a nonhostile, nonthreatening environment a lack of respect, or is it, rather, the very essence of respect? That is a question we must contemplate.

I call *Miranda* the triumph of formalism. In my judgment, *Miranda* should be repudiated. It's bad constitutional law. It's ill-conceived policy. And most grievous, it has created a jurisprudence of formalism.

With *Miranda,* appellate and trial courts are forced to decipher and apply rigid principles—often with no consideration of the Fifth Amendment's underlying concern with compulsion. We have come to the point where actual coercion isn't even the issue.

The irrelevance of actual compulsion is illustrated by the case of *United States* v. *Dockery*. Francine Dockery worked in a bank. After she was accused by a coworker of embezzling bank funds, FBI agents requested bank officials to summon her to a small, vacant office in the bank. The agents told Dockery that she did not have to answer questions, that she was not under arrest, and that she was free to leave at any time. The agents then lied to Dockery and told her that they had her fingerprints and believed she was involved in the thefts. When she persisted in denying her involvement, the agents terminated the interview, which had lasted sixteen minutes, and asked her to wait in a reception area.

A few minutes later, Dockery asked to talk to the agents again. The agents then repeated the advice they had previously given her, and she again denied involvement in the crime. When the agents said they doubted she was telling the truth, she finally implicated herself in the crime.

According to Professor Joseph Grano, "under almost any standard of voluntariness, it is inconceivable that *Dockery* would have required much judicial time. While the agents' false statement might raise a judicial eyebrow, by itself the deception was insufficient to render the defendant's responses involuntary."

Nevertheless, *Dockery* became a troubling case for the Court because of the issue of what constitutes custody. It was ultimately determined that Dockery could legitimately be considered in custody because her employer asked her to meet with the FBI and the FBI had asked her to wait in a reception area after the first interview.

This may seem like a convoluted way to define "custody," but the case of Richard Mesa was even more absurd.

FBI agents with an arrest warrant surrounded a motel in which Mesa, who had shot and wounded his wife and daughter the previous day, had barricaded himself. The FBI blocked his means of escape. Believing that he was armed and not knowing whether or not he held hostages, they decided against the use of force. Mesa did not respond to calls to surrender, and agents obtained an FBI hostage negotiator and persuaded Mesa to accept a mobile phone.

Mesa and the hostage negotiator talked on the phone for three hours. Mesa did most of the talking. In long, rambling monologues, he spoke of his childhood, his war experiences, and of his relationship with his wife and daughter. The negotiator, knowing of Mesa's psychiatric history and fearing suicide, made supportive comments, hoping to gain his trust.

Finally, Mesa surrendered, and he was given his *Miranda* warning for the first time. He thanked the negotiator for listening and said he would have certainly killed himself if it were not for the negotiator. During the trial, the court concluded that "custodial interrogation" had occurred while the negotiator was talking to Mesa. When the case went before the court of appeals, the judges struggled—and failed—to find common ground. One judge said that this was not like station house custody, that the FBI didn't have control over Mesa, and that Mesa's inability to leave the hotel room did not make the situation custodial. Furthermore, Mesa's statements to the negotiator were voluntary. A second judge agreed that the conversation was not interrogation, but disagreed about the custody issue. He felt Mesa's situation *did* amount to custody. The third judge dissented on both counts. He stated that Mesa was in custody, that his conversation with the negotiator constituted interrogation, and that anything he said, no matter how voluntary, should be disregarded. So you see, there is no agreement among legal experts on the boundaries of the law. That in itself should be cause for alarm.

A 1984 New York case, *People* v. *Ferro,* offers a horrifying example of the formalism that has evolved around *Miranda.* Alfio Ferro was arrested for a residential robbery of furs that turned into a murder. While in custody, Ferro asked a detective if he could speak to the district attorney, but dropped the request when the detective indicated that Ferro would have to first tell the detective what he planned to say. The detective then left but returned moments later carrying the furs that he had obtained from a codefendant's apartment. Without saying a word, the detective placed the furs in front of Ferro's cell. Believing the detective had information that he'd committed the crime, Ferro then made incriminating statements. He was convicted of murder, but his conviction was overturned on appeal. According to the appellate court, the detective who interrogated Ferro should have known that Ferro was reasonably likely to respond to his placing the furs in front of him.

To say that the detective's action was compulsion is, frankly, insane. We let a convicted murderer go free for *this*? Liberal or conservative, any *thinking* person should be deeply offended by the result.

What's the solution? I am growing increasingly convinced that the first step should be to overrule *Miranda.* Professors Grano and Caplan have recommended such a course. I know that's a very controversial position to take. There is a concern that overruling *Miranda* might be perceived as a license to the police to resume abusive practices. This concern about appropriate police behavior is always valid, but I believe that *Miranda* is the wrong means to the end we are seeking.

Make no mistake about it, says Grano, "*Miranda* does not have the virtue of furthering good policy. On the contrary, its antipathy to police interrogation and self-incrimination undermines . . . legitimate and weighty societal interests in law enforcement. Its ideology sits as a time bomb waiting to be triggered by a more sympathetic court."

These are the reasons *Miranda* should be overruled:

- *Miranda* is not a wise or necessary decision—nor a harmless one.
- *Miranda* has sent our jurisprudence on a hazardous detour by introducing novel conceptions of the proper relationship between a criminal suspect and a law enforcement officer.
- *Miranda* has accentuated just those features in our system that manifest the *least* regard for truth-seeking: the view that the process is a game of chance in which the defendant should always have some prospect of victory.
- *Miranda* was decided at a time when effective alternatives for restraining unlawful police conduct were ripe for implementation but were subsequently never pursued.
- The meaning of *Miranda* has not become reasonably clear, as its advocates contend. Rather, technical issues continue to abound about its meaning and scope.

Miranda's rigidity has led to judicial chaos. All too often, courts have saved some perfectly voluntary confessions only by straining *Miranda* to the breaking point. At the same time, other courts have been willing to suppress statements that were clearly voluntary.

The survival of conviction for serious crimes has not depended on whether the Fifth Amendment was violated but in which of the above approaches the courts indulged.

There is no reason to fear that overruling *Miranda* will return us to the Dark Ages of police abuse. As long as we are firm in our judicial commitment to freedom and the protection of citizens' rights, we will achieve results that are honest and fair. The key is the practice, not the formality.

| 4 |

CLAM UP AND CALL YOUR LAWYER

The Right to Counsel and
the Rules of Investigation

> For the police to seal the defendant's fate by obtain-
> ing evidence from the defendant's mouth . . . is some-
> how supposed to leave us with a sense of unfairness,
> with a sense that the rules of fair play have been vio-
> lated.
>
> PROFESSOR JOSEPH D. GRANO

On the morning of June 22, 1975, the bludgeoned body of
Diane Snell was found off North French Road in the town of
Amherst, in upstate New York. Police attention focused
almost immediately upon Joseph Skinner, who had been seen
talking with Snell in a local bar the previous night. Two days
after the murder, Skinner was twice questioned by Amherst
detectives. He admitted that he'd spoken to Snell in the bar,
but that was all. The police asked Skinner if he'd take a lie
detector test, and he agreed. The results made the police

more suspicious than ever, but after much questioning, Skinner continued to protest that he had nothing to do with Snell's murder. However, during a second polygraph interview, Skinner finally acknowledged that he had given Snell a ride from the bar to the Riverside section of Buffalo.

The police asked Skinner to drive with them along the same route, and he agreed. But the journey produced nothing, and it ended when Skinner asked to be taken home.

Skinner was getting agitated by the continued police questioning, so he hired a lawyer, Leo Fallon. The first thing Fallon told him was, "You don't have to talk to the cops." Then Fallon called the department and told the investigators that he represented Skinner and they could no longer question his client outside his presence. As so often happens, that put a lid on the questioning. And it effectively ended the investigation—or so it seemed. Behind the scenes, police continued to work the open file and look for leads. In March 1977, eighteen months later, they came upon a potential witness and wanted Skinner back for a lineup.

The first thing the police did was contact Fallon's office with an order to show cause as to why his client should not be compelled to appear in the lineup. But they also served Skinner personally.

When Skinner opened his door to find Detectives Mark Hohensee and Ed Meredith on the steps, he was immediately upset. He signed the order, but his agitation increased. "Why do I have to appear in a lineup?" he demanded. He'd assumed the investigation was dead.

"Call your lawyer. He'll explain it," Hohensee replied.

But Skinner did not calm down. Sensing there was something to be explored, Hohensee asked him if he wanted to talk about the Snell murder. "If you're involved, you might want to get it off your chest once and for all," he said quietly.

Skinner seemed to collapse in on himself. "Okay, I'll talk," he said, and led the detectives inside.

Hohensee read the *Miranda* warnings, then Skinner began to speak, making a number of damaging admissions. After a while, Skinner agreed to be taken to police headquarters, but once there he seemed to have second thoughts. He refused to make a formal statement until he had spoken with his attorney, and the police did not question him further.

Skinner was eventually charged with the murder of Diane Snell and went to trial, where the incriminating statements he'd made to the two detectives were admitted. He was convicted of manslaughter in the first degree. The New York Court of Appeals, however, reversed the conviction.

The court held that in retaining counsel, Skinner had unequivocally indicated that he felt himself unable to deal with the authorities without legal assistance, and that his right to counsel was "indelible"—that is, he could not waive counsel without counsel being present.

The New York Court of Appeals did not show any concern about balancing the needs of society with those of the individual. "Indelible" is one of those words that substitutes for thought. It suggests final, fundamental, unchangeable, not to be questioned. It is not argument or analysis. It is fiat.

This was a five-to-two decision, and Judge Matthew Jasen, one of the dissenters, protested vehemently:

The majority has today created *an entirely new rule of law,* to wit: that one who is suspected of having committed a crime and who is not in custody, not indicted, not arraigned and not even formally accused by anyone, cannot waive his right to counsel, after being advised of his constitutional rights, in the comfort and quiet of his own home in the presence of police officers whom he himself invited to remain there. The purported legal basis for such a rule is that the suspect's right to counsel had somehow "indelibly" attached merely because the defendant had retained an attorney to counsel him during the ongoing investigation. In my opinion, such a rule is not supported by logic, common sense, need or the prior decisions of this court and I cannot support its acceptance into the law of this State.

Jasen's concern was with the question of when the right to counsel attaches. And his moral outrage was justified by the fact that Skinner's conviction was reversed on a technicality of law that did not seem reasonable in the first place. In effect, the law suggested that a defendant could not be trusted to know or speak his own mind without an attorney present.

This absurdly broad definition of the right to counsel was not always the law. It is the result of decades of generous interpretation of the Sixth Amendment.

The Sixth Amendment provides that "In all criminal prosecutions, the accused shall enjoy the right . . . to have the assistance of counsel for his defense." I have no quarrel with the idea that the right to counsel is an essential component of the right to a fair trial. But I will argue that the Sixth Amendment provides no right to counsel during police interrogation. In theory—and, too often, in practice—when suspects don't speak to police, the investigation is short-circuited. We have taken a constitutional right at trial and expanded it to the police station and beyond.

The Sixth Amendment was adopted in response to English law, which, until 1836, did not provide felony defendants the right even to have retained counsel assist them in presenting a defense at trial. After the American Revolution, most of the states rejected the English law, and some even granted unrepresented defendants a right to appointed counsel—something England did not provide until 1903.

It wasn't until 1938, in *Johnson* v. *Zerbst,* that the U.S. Supreme Court held that the Sixth Amendment afforded indigent defendants a right to appointed counsel in the federal courts. And it wasn't until 1963 that the U.S. Supreme Court held, in *Gideon* v. *Wainwright,* that the Sixth and Fourteenth Amendments required such appointment of counsel for indigent defendants in felony cases in the state courts.

All of this was long overdue—and to be welcomed. There can be no fair trial without counsel. It is also clear why the right to counsel was expanded to include pretrial hearings and a period of preparation. A defendant who meets his lawyer the day he appears in court cannot be said to have had "counsel."

This principle, that after formal proceedings have commenced an accused has a Sixth Amendment right to counsel at "critical stages" of the criminal proceedings, is derived from *Powell* v. *Alabama,* a U.S. Supreme Court case decided in 1932, sometimes referred to as the Scottsboro case.

In the Scottsboro case, several black men were charged with raping two white women on a freight train. The defendants were severed into three groups. They were arrested on March 25, 1931, indicted and arraigned on March 31, and the trials began on April 6. Each of the three trials was completed within a single day. All of the defendants were found guilty and sentenced to death.

The judgment was reversed by the U.S. Supreme Court because the defendants did not have the aid of counsel until the very day they appeared in court. The decision was based on the rationale that an unaided layman needs assistance in the preparation and presentation of his case and in coping with procedural complexities in order to assure a fair trial. The Court said: "The right to be heard would be, in many cases, of little avail if it did not comprehend the right to be heard by counsel."

So, in determining whether a stage of the proceedings is a "critical" one at which the defendant is entitled to a lawyer, it is important to recognize that the theoretical foundation of the Sixth Amendment right to counsel is based on the traditional role of an attorney as a legal expert and strategist.

I would, however, argue forcefully that we have taken this "right" too far. Where a defendant has been provided with counsel and has had an opportunity to confer with him (and where the defense attorney has undoubtedly told the defendant not to talk to anyone without the attorney being present), there is simply no constitutional prohibition against the use of incriminating information *voluntarily* obtained from an accused despite the fact that his attorney may not be present. In those circumstances the defendant has been informed of his rights by his attorney, and often he has been informed of his *Miranda* rights by the police.

Once the accused has been made aware of his rights, is it not *his* responsibility to decide whether or not to exercise them? If he *voluntarily* relinquishes his rights by talking to the police, or if he decides to disclose incriminating evidence to someone he mistakenly trusts or believes will not report it to the police, he should be responsible for his actions and bear the adverse consequences that result. It is common sense. More than that, it is a respect for the individual's fundamental autonomy and freedom to choose to speak.

How did we come from the point of requiring the assistance of counsel at trial to a situation where the represented defendant—or even the suspect—is sacred and immune from police investigation? And when did the absence of counsel make a suspect's confession worthless?

Prior to 1958, the U.S. Supreme Court had *never* indicated that a denial of counsel to a suspect was sufficient by itself to render a confession inadmissible. It had consistently held that lack of counsel was merely a factor in determining voluntariness. But in 1964, that changed. In *Massiah* v. *United States,* the U.S. Supreme Court held that once a person has been indicted or formally charged, he has a right to counsel. Unless that person voluntarily and knowingly waives that right, *any* incriminating statement he makes in the absence of his attorney *must* be excluded—if the statement has been deliberately elicited from him by a government agent.

The ruling that would shake the foundation of the Sixth Amendment occurred this way:

Winston Massiah was a seaman on a Grace Lines ship. Beginning in 1956, he, along with two of his shipmates, became involved in the cocaine trade, obtaining the cocaine in Valparaiso, Chile, concealing it on the ship, and bringing it to New York. In New York, they passed the cocaine along to two other men who distributed it. Between 1956 and 1959, at least twelve shiploads were distributed.

In May 1958, customs agents boarded Massiah's ship when it docked in New York and found five packages of cocaine weighing over three and a half pounds. Massiah was arrested, and three weeks later he was indicted for possessing the drugs. He was released on bail. In July 1959, Massiah was again indicted together with Jesse Colson, one of his New York distributors, and charged with conspiracy. Both men were released on bail pending trial.

Unbeknownst to Massiah, Colson decided to cooperate with the government and wear a taping device during a pre-arranged meeting with Massiah. On the evening of November 19, 1959, Massiah entered Colson's car on West 146th Street between Seventh and Eighth Avenues. As the two men sat together in the car, Massiah made statements to Colson that fully implicated him and left no doubt of his guilt.

At Massiah's trial, his attorney sought to suppress the evidence of his statements on the grounds that he was under indictment at the time and was represented by counsel. Therefore, it was a denial of his right to counsel for any government agent to procure and listen to his conversation with Colson unless his lawyer was present.

The trial judge and the court of appeals disagreed. The court of appeals held that the government had the duty to continue its investigation of the possible criminal activities of those suspected of the crime, even though they might be under indictment. Massiah acquired no immunity from the government's procuring additional evidence "merely by reason of having retained an attorney." Indeed, the court of appeals held that "the public interest would clearly seem to require the continuance" of the investigations of this large-scale conspiracy "so that all involved may be prosecuted."

It was not disputed that Massiah entered the car of his own free will and that he was free to speak about the case or to say nothing.

Massiah took his appeal to the U.S. Supreme Court. The solicitor general, who argued on behalf of the government, was Archibald Cox, later of Watergate fame. Cox stressed in his brief: "This case does not involve either coercion or the potentiality of coercion. Massiah was not questioned by anyone who even appeared to be a government agent; rather, his 'interrogator' was his own partner in crime, to whom he talked freely. Massiah was, of course, under no police control or restraint at the time and was free to come and go as he pleased."

Cox asserted convincingly that "there is no problem of physical or psychological compulsion or the threat of coercion; . . . indeed, and perhaps most important of all, the defendant was not in custody, not even in the loose and inaccurate sense in which one may be in custody when he's in the district attorney's office being questioned even though he's not under arrest. He was free to come and go as he chose. . . ."

The Court disagreed. In a remarkably brief opinion, the Supreme Court reversed Massiah's conviction on May 1, 1964, by a six-to-three vote.

The Court held that Massiah was denied his right to counsel when at his trial his incriminating words, which federal agents had "deliberately elicited" from him after indictment and in the absence of counsel, were used against him. This rule, the Court said, applies to "indirect and surreptitious interrogations" as well as those conducted at a police station or in a jail.

The Court's dissenters feared that the ruling would jeopardize all police interrogation and make it virtually impossible for the police to do their job. "A civilized society must maintain its capacity to discover transgressions of the law and to identify those who flout it," wrote Justice Byron White. "It is, therefore, a rather portentous occasion when a constitutional rule is established barring the use of evidence which is relevant, reliable, and highly probative of the issue which the trial court has before it—whether the accused committed the act. Without the evidence, the quest for truth may be seriously impeded."

Sadly, White observed, the Court had created "another area of privileged testimony" and "additional barriers to the pursuit of truth."

The irony is, under *Massiah,* defendants who have had access to counsel—and, therefore, who presumably *know* their rights—are provided greater protection than those who are without counsel and may not know of their rights. If Colson had obtained or elicited the statements from Massiah prior to indictment or arraignment, the statements would have been admissible without question. In fact, Colson deceived not only Massiah, but another codefendant, Greg Anfield, as well. Nobody argued that Anfield's right to counsel had been violated, because the Colson-Anfield meeting occurred *before* he had been indicted.

In 1980, the U.S. Supreme Court, in *United States* v. *Henry,* applied the *Massiah* ruling in a different setting but in analogous circumstances.

In 1972, Billy Gale Henry and two others, while wearing masks and carrying guns, robbed a bank in Norfolk, Virginia. No witnesses were able to identify any of the men. However, as a result of finding a rent receipt in the abandoned getaway car, government agents were able to arrest Henry some three months later. Henry was incarcerated and the indictment followed two weeks later.

Shortly thereafter, government agents investigating the robbery contacted Jeff Nichols, a paid informant who was then serving a sentence on a forgery conviction. Nichols told the government agent that he was housed in the same cell block as Henry, and the agent told Nichols to be "alert" to any statements made by Henry—but not to initiate any conversation with or question Henry about the bank robbery. Nichols was released from jail within two weeks and informed the government that Henry had told him about the robbery. (Henry had *also* asked Nichols to get him a floor plan of the U.S. Marshal's office and a handcuff key because he intended to attempt an escape.)

Nichols testified at Henry's trial, and Henry was found guilty and sentenced to twenty-five years.

The U.S. Supreme Court reversed the conviction. It made no difference that Henry had not been questioned. Nor did the Supreme Court inquire as to whether Henry or Nichols first raised the subject of the robbery. It was enough for the court that (1) Nichols was a paid informant acting for the government, (2) Henry did not know this, and (3) Henry was in custody and under indictment when he conversed with Nichols.

Justice Harry Blackmun wrote, in a sarcastic dissent: "I cannot believe that *Massiah* requires exclusion when a cellmate previously unknown to the defendant and asked only to keep his ears open says: 'It's a nice day,' and the defendant responds: 'It would be nicer if I hadn't robbed that bank' . . . and this court does not show that anything more transpired."

We must understand that our affection for formalism in the law has dire consequences that stab at the heart of our most precious moral values. Consider the case of Perley Moulton.

Perley Moulton and a codefendant, Gary Colson (no relation to the *Massiah* Colson) were indicted on several felony counts of theft after receiving stolen property in April 1981. In November 1982 (the long time span is not explained), Colson called the Belfast, Maine, police chief to say he wanted to talk about the case. The chief cautioned Colson to consult with his attorney before saying more.

Two days later, without further contact with the police, Colson met with Moulton. At that meeting, Moulton spoke of "getting rid of a couple of witnesses," including Gary Elwell, a key prosecution witness. Moulton had formed a general plan for the murder and Colson's role was to pick up a car to be used in the murder.

Four days later, Colson met with the police at the office of his attorney and told the police of Moulton's plan to kill Elwell. The police knew that several witnesses in the case had already received threats. One witness had been personally threatened by Moulton, and another had been told, "A cup of acid could be thrown in your face" if he talked to the police.

Colson then consented to have the police place a recording device on his home phone, since Moulton planned to call Colson when the arrangements to kill Elwell had been finalized.

Three telephone calls, all initiated by Moulton, were subsequently recorded. During the calls, Moulton referred to the plan to kill Elwell and discussed a fabricated story that he planned to use at trial. Finally, Moulton said he wanted to meet with Colson to "review the whole plan."

At the request of the police, Colson agreed to wear a body recorder/transmitter during this meeting. The purpose of the device was to learn more about the plan to kill the witness and also to ensure Colson's safety.

The police told Colson, "Act like yourself, converse normally, and *avoid* trying to draw information out of Moulton."

During the meeting, without any prompting by Colson, Moulton brought up the possibility of killing Elwell by means of an air gun with hollow-tipped darts or explosives, and also suggested developing false testimony for presentation at trial. These portions of the transcript were not admitted at Moulton's trial, but there was also discussion of the thefts and these portions *were* admitted. Moulton was convicted.

The U.S. Supreme Court, however, held that Moulton's Sixth Amendment right to counsel was violated by the admission at trial of his incriminating statements to Colson after indictment and at the meeting of the two "to plan defense strategy" at the trial. Once the right to counsel has attached, the state must honor it. There is no merit to the argument that the statements obtained by the police should not be suppressed because the police had other, legitimate reasons for listening to the defendant's conversations with Colson, namely to investigate the defendant's plan to kill the witness and to ensure Colson's safety.

Justice Warren Burger, in dissent, found this result "bizarre," as do I. Burger noted that the U.S. Supreme Court had created a new "right" for "habitual offenders who persist in criminal activity even while under indictment for other crimes."

It is clear that the statements obtained by Colson *could* have been used against the defendant at a subsequent trial for crimes apart from those on which the defendant had already been indicted—such as conspiracy to commit murder and obstruction of justice. It would seem that the state engaged in no impermissible conduct. Indeed, the police would have been derelict in their duty if they had failed to follow up on Colson's information—and subject to censure if they had failed to protect him when he endangered his life.

As Burger wrote with a note of disgust, "It is a judicial aberration conferring a windfall benefit" on those who pursue other crimes while out on bail for those crimes they have already committed. It turns the Sixth Amendment into a "magic cloak" to protect criminals.

It seems to me the question is a simple one: What is the practical distinction between what occurs in the police station and what occurs in the trial court?

In the police station the defendant is not confronted with legal procedures and rules but with questions of fact relating to his involvement in a crime. Police interrogation is an investigative tool for obtaining evidence—like a search or a blood test. The Sixth Amendment was not intended to help a defendant protect himself against the possibility that the investigation will succeed. If interrogation does not result in an involuntary confession, the law should regard it the same way it does a lawful search.

As Professor Grano has noted, "The *only* constitutional rule that applies in the police station is the one that precludes the police from *compelling* the defendant to answer questions." When counsel tells a defendant not to make a voluntary statement, he is doing more than enforcing that rule. As Judge Henry J. Friendly, chief justice of the U.S. Court of Appeals, Second Circuit, once said, "there is no social value in preventing uncoerced admission of the facts." And nothing in the Sixth Amendment's history compels us to accept this as its goal or purpose.

Some would argue that ours is an adversarial or accusatorial system, and that counsel is the "equalizer" who gives the defendant parity with the state—and that therefore counsel should be free to interfere with the government's efforts to obtain information against the defendant.

However, although adversarial balance, or rough equality, may be the norm that dictates trial procedures, it has never been the norm that dictates the rules of investigation and the gathering of proof.

I would contend that a right to have counsel's assistance in trying to avoid unwise self-incrimination during police interrogation cannot be justified by the Sixth Amendment's text, historical purpose, or sound policy. That being the case, what was the Supreme Court's basis for applying the Sixth Amendment to police interrogations that take place after the start of adversary judicial proceedings against the accused?

As noted by Professor Grano, Justice Potter Stewart was the architect of this position. Stewart argued that the Constitution structured the criminal justice system into two distinct phases. In the *investigative* phase the police have considerable leeway as long as they do not coerce the defendant. In the *judicial* phase, which marks the end of the investigative phase, the police may not approach the defendant unless they do so in a way that accords with the procedural protections of the accusatorial judicial process. So, after arraignment or indictment, the police may not contact the defendant without counsel's involvement.

"If Stewart's arguments were valid, searches and seizures after the start of adversary judicial proceedings would seem as impermissible as police interrogation," wrote Grano, adding that courts have *not* barred postcharge searches, "and Stewart never explained why the Sixth, not the Fifth, should be viewed as barring only efforts to elicit evidence from the defendant's mouth." This kind of inconsistent thought process makes law a lottery.

In New York, where I sit on the bench, the courts have chosen to go far beyond the U.S. Supreme Court, and every other state in the nation, in holding that an individual who has obtained counsel on a matter under investigation may *not* be interrogated by the police on that subject, even in a noncustodial setting, after the defendant's attorney has told the police not to question the defendant in his absence. As recently as 1993, the New York Court of Appeals reversed another murder conviction—that of a known drug dealer and killer—on this basis.

Victor West was convicted of second-degree murder in the execution-style shooting of Lawrence Coleman, a stranger to West. West shot him in the head in a fit of anger because Coleman had parked on the street in a spot West had reserved for his own use to sell drugs.

In June 1982, four months after the homicide, West was placed in a lineup in connection with the shooting. He was represented at that time by counsel, and his counsel's presence was noted in the police file. The attorney told the police not to question West in his absence. The results of the lineup were inconclusive and West was not charged at that time.

A full three years later, police arrested Dave Davenport, who had been involved in West's drug operation, on charges unrelated to the Coleman homicide. Davenport admitted his involvement in the Coleman homicide, identified West as the shooter, and agreed to surreptitiously tape conversations with West in exchange for leniency. The police did not, at the time, attempt to determine whether West was still represented by counsel with respect to the Coleman homicide. Thereafter, West made incriminating statements to Davenport, which were taped.

At trial, West's attorney sought to exclude the statements taped by Davenport, contending that they were taken in violation of his client's right to counsel. The district attorney responded that, more than three years after the lineup, they had no reason to believe that the representation continued. West did not even allege that he was in fact still represented at the time the tape recordings were made. The trial court denied the motion and West was convicted of murder. The appellate division agreed, finding that the investigation for which West had obtained counsel had been terminated and that the taped statements were part of a new investigation. The court also found it significant that the taped statements were made in a noncustodial setting. But the New York Court of Appeals disagreed and reversed the conviction.

The court found that the right to counsel applied whether or not the defendant had established that he was still represented by counsel at the time of the taping. The police had the burden to determine whether or not representation in fact continued, although how they were supposed to do that is left unanswered. The defendant had no obligation to keep the police informed as to the status of the attorney-client relationship. The mere passage of three years did not eradicate the defendant's indelible right to counsel.

Mind you, the court did not hold that the right to counsel is interminable. If the police had reason to believe that the defendant's attorney had died or been disbarred, its holding might have been different.

Once again, a murderer went free, sliding down the slippery slope of our court's formalism. We have to ask if this is the result we want from our constitutional protections—that a career drug dealer and murderer can hide behind the cloak of the very law he flaunts daily.

| 5 |

THE RUSH TO NOWHERE

Speedy Trial Statutes Do Not
Guarantee Rapid Justice

Make haste slowly.
LATIN PROVERB

In the early evening of November 16, 1973, Herbert Hilton, a convicted felon out on parole, assaulted Wendell Thomas, striking him with a baseball bat, then stealing his watch and cash. Hilton was arrested and charged with the violent felonies of assault and robbery. Despite the severity of the crime and his record, Hilton was released on bail.

Several months later, Hilton, his lawyer, and the district attorney appeared in the New York criminal court. The DA's office stated that it was ready for trial, in keeping with the speedy trial statute. At that point, Hilton whispered to his attorney that he had to make a phone call. He walked out of the court and never returned.

A warrant was issued for Hilton's arrest, and during the next eight months both the Warrant Squad of the police department and the State Department of Parole made at least nine separate and unsuccessful attempts to locate and arrest Hilton.

It was eight years before Hilton appeared in the system again—this time arrested on local charges in Charlotte, North Carolina. North Carolina notified the New York Department of Parole, and Hilton was returned to New York and remanded for a parole violation. None of the parties were aware that Hilton had an outstanding bench warrant on the assault charge, and Hilton certainly didn't call it to their attention.

Two more years passed, and Hilton was released on parole and arrested again—this time in Suffolk County, New York, for driving while intoxicated. At that point, ten years after the fact, the sheriff discovered the outstanding 1974 bench warrant, and Hilton was returned to New York County to stand trial.

Somewhat disingenuously, Hilton's attorney moved to dismiss the indictment on the grounds that Hilton had been "denied" his right to a speedy trial. The trial court said no, noting that the district attorney had been ready for trial in 1974, and that Hilton abdicated his claim to a speedy trial when he disappeared. The trial went ahead, and a jury convicted Hilton of assault in the first degree. He was sentenced to a term of imprisonment of four to eight years.

Hilton appealed the conviction solely on the basis that he had been denied a speedy trial. And in June 1989, in its "ultimate wisdom," the appellate court reversed Hilton's conviction. While the court did not deny that the People had been ready in 1974, it stated that Hilton should have been prosecuted when he was arrested eight years later, and that the two-year delay resulted in an infringement of his right to a speedy trial.

The opinion of the court was brief and matter-of-fact. It evidenced no distress at being compelled to arrive at such an absurd decision. It reflected no awareness of the incongruity and plain foolishness of such a result.

The court could have found that Hilton, by fleeing for eight years and then failing to notify authorities of his pending case when he was rearrested, had forfeited his right to a speedy trial. It is clear, for example, that when Hilton fled on the morning his trial was scheduled to begin, he waived his right to be present at his trial. He could have been tried in absentia.

The law was not designed to "protect" a person who would flaunt it. Hilton, after all, was not a novice unfamiliar with the ways of criminal justice. He was a repeat felon who played the system, seeming to abide by the rules until the moment of truth arrived. Why should he be let off the hook?

I am very much in favor of an accused citizen having the right to a speedy trial. Yet I look at a case like this and wonder how we have come to this pitiful point. The only consolation, I suppose, is that it took the appellate court four years to decide that Hilton's right to a speedy trial had been denied—and Hilton spent those four years in jail. Apparently, Hilton didn't have the right to a speedy *appeal*!

The *Hilton* case is not the exception. It is the rule. It reflects the increasingly arcane, intricate, technical, and complex nature of our law. This mass of rules grows like a fungus, developing a life of its own. Ultimately, it turns in on itself and consumes its own flesh—making a mockery of the very rights it is designed to protect.

Speedy trial is guaranteed by the Sixth Amendment, applied to the states through the due process clause of the Fourteenth Amendment. The right to a speedy trial has a threefold purpose: it protects an accused person who is jailed pending trial against prolonged imprisonment; it relieves the accused person of the anxiety and public suspicion that accompanies being accused of a crime; and it prevents an accused person from the hazards of a trial after a long delay—for example, loss of witnesses or dulling of memory.

There is also a societal interest in prompt and certain justice. The people deserve to have a criminal brought to justice with due speed.

But there are two complicating factors. First, the courts do not consider the matter of a speedy trial in a vacuum, but rather in the context of all surrounding circumstances. Clearly, some causes of delay may be considered more justifiable than others.

Second, as we all know, delay is frequently employed as a tactic by the defense for a number of purposes that work to the advantage of the defendant. So a delay is not necessarily prejudicial against the accused.

In interpreting the constitutional right to a speedy trial, the Supreme Court has articulated criteria to be balanced in determining when the right has been violated.

The precedent is a four-factor test:

- Length of delay
- Reason for delay
- Whether and how the defendant asserted his right
- Prejudice to the defendant with regard to possible impairment of the defense

When the Criminal Procedure Law was first enacted in New York in 1971, the commission decided not to attempt to define a speedy trial in terms of fixed time limitations because it seemed impossible to apply a general principle to every unique situation that might arise. The commission concluded that speedy trial was such an elastic and elusive concept that its meaning could best be determined judicially on a case-by-case basis—or that if specific time periods were feasible these should be determined by special study and action of a specialized legislative or administrative agency devoted exclusively to that task.

In the late 1960s and early 1970s, the U.S. Congress along with many state legislatures undertook the task of producing highly technical statutes with rigid speedy trial requirements that relied on mathematical computations and strict time limits for determining what constitutes a speedy trial.

The impetus behind these efforts was a concern over continuing court congestion and the fear that the judicial branch was unwilling or unable to deal with it.

The approach of the New York legislature was typical of the recklessness of this pursuit. The commission set up to deal with revisions in criminal procedure recommended that before the legislature pulled a statute out of its hat detailing specific time periods, there should first be a study by a committee devoted solely to that task. The legislature ignored that sensible recommendation and established a statutory time period in 1972. In the decades since, there has never been a review to find out if the statute has served its intended purpose of reducing delay and promoting speedy trials. As with so much "reform" legislation, it simply became a part of the jurisprudential landscape. We neither anticipated its impact nor dealt with its consequences.

Speedy trial rules do not govern the time within which a trial must commence. They deal only with the subject of when the People must be ready for trial. The fact that the People are ready to proceed does not mean the trial is at hand. Various other factors might result in a delay. However, if the People fail to comply with the statute, the case will be dismissed without regard to whether that failure actually delayed the trial.

Every day, thousands of men and women are seeking justice in our courts—as are victims, the families of victims, and the state. We struggle with limited resources, human and material, and the sheer impossibility of providing balanced, efficient justice for all. High-minded concepts like speedy trial often get shoved aside, which produces one terrible result: Criminals go free because justice could not be delivered swiftly, according to arbitrary standards.

There is no question that the idea of a speedy trial is a good one. It would be a miscarriage of justice to detain defendants for an unreasonable period of time prior to trial. This right also bears in mind that the longer the delay, the weaker the case; witnesses may disappear, memories fade.

But this does not take into account the terrible congestion that afflicts our courts. And rather than address the issue of congestion, our government has chosen to tunnel its vision and resolve the matter with a rigid set of rules that often doesn't lead to a just result.

One of the craziest outcomes of the speedy trial rules is the latitude given defendants who escape justice. Fernando Luperon was charged with attempted murder after he wounded his New York landlord in a shooting incident. He was released on his own recognizance two days later, but he failed to appear on the scheduled court date. A bench warrant was issued for his arrest.

Luperon was arrested two months later on unrelated charges, at which time the outstanding bench warrant was discovered. Again, he was released on his own recognizance, and again he failed to appear on scheduled court dates. A year went by.

When Luperon was finally rearrested and brought to court, his attorney argued that the charges should be dropped because of the "inexcusable delay" in bringing Luperon to trial. The attorney's argument was that the People did not use due diligence in finding Luperon and rearresting him after he failed to appear in court. The court denied this motion and Luperon was brought to trial and convicted.

The conviction, however, was reversed by the appellate court on speedy trial grounds. In essence, the court decreed that the police should have tried harder to locate Luperon during the period he was missing. The onus was on the state to bring him to trial, whether Luperon himself was interested in speedy justice or not. It's simply absurd.

The irony of the speedy trial rules is that most defendants and defense attorneys don't *want* a speedy trial. Delay usually benefits a guilty defendant, and most defendants held for trial are guilty of some or all of the charges against them.

Philip Conner was another successful manipulator of the system. Conner was arrested and charged with assault in the second degree and thereafter released on bail. The district attorney subsequently informed Conner's attorney that he had been indicted, and the defense attorney selected the date when he and Conner would appear for arraignment. They arrived that morning and were told that the case would not be called until later that afternoon. Since Conner's attorney had other cases to attend to, they left the courtroom. It is quite common for defense attorneys to have numerous cases calendared in different court parts on the same day.

Conner's case was again adjourned to a mutually agreeable date. On that date, however, Conner's attorney was on trial in another matter and he sent his law partner in his stead.

Conner and his attorney slid into a back row of the court-room and sat there without informing anyone of their presence. Strictly speaking, this is legal; ethically, it's questionable. At the very least, it's a form of game playing that many defense attorneys engage in. It worked for Conner. Inadvertently, Conner's case was not called.

The two delays in Conner's case were charged to the state, and because they exceeded by three days the six-month speedy trial provision, the indictment was dismissed. Conner walked.

Conner is a winner in our criminal justice sweepstakes, which operates without regard to the seriousness of the charges or the quality of evidence against a defendant. If Conner or his attorneys had wanted a speedy trial he could have had his case called on either of the dates that he appeared. Instead, he contrived for his own convenience and that of his attorneys to obtain a delay. In our heavily burdened system, the prosecutor and the courts are required to perform perfectly and without flaw. Nothing at all is required of the defendant.

We have become engaged in a search for error, in which the issue of a defendant's guilt is irrelevant. We are exalting arbitrariness. We don't ask, Has the defendant been deprived of his right to a speedy trial? We don't evaluate the proper factors that would give us a meaningful answer. We just count the days and that's it. If the defendant is wily enough, he can let the clock run out.

I recently had a case before me that I had adjourned to a "date certain for hearing and trial." On that date, an associate of the defense attorney appeared and informed me that the defense attorney was on vacation. I was told that when she returned, she would need additional time to prepare her case. The associate requested one month. The district attorney, however, reported that he would be ready for trial in two days.

The defense attorney seized upon the "two days" with impassioned indignation, calling for those two days to be charged to the state. Although it was the defendant who had requested a monthlong delay, I had to endure a lengthy, petty, and irrelevant statement about some fictional abridgment of the defendant's rights.

I must tell you, I am not exhilarated by such discussions. They demean our system. Surely, advocacy should be more than this pettiness.

In the period of time since these speedy trial statutes have been relied upon, there has not been a single study that has demonstrated that such rigid time limits have made the system more efficient or been effective in protecting defendants' rights. If anything, case processing has been prolonged by speedy trial motions and hearings.

Why do we do this to ourselves? The Constitution does not require it. It creates more problems than it solves. It doesn't work. Sadly, it only adds to the cynicism with which many defendants already regard the system. Defendants charged with vicious and violent crimes, where the evidence of guilt is strong and compelling, often have the charges against them dismissed without regard for their guilt. Defense attorneys who may not even want a speedy trial are encouraged to manipulate the system.

It is now entirely possible—and may even be probable—that an accused person might have the charges against him dismissed on speedy trial grounds, even though he has been provided with a speedy trial as required by the Constitution, because the rigid time requirements of these statutes have not been strictly followed. Examples of this abound.

Joseph Jones, a predicate felon (meaning he had previous convictions), was accused of selling cocaine to an undercover policeman and of possessing a large quantity of the drug at the time of his arrest. Shortly after his arrest, Jones made bail and promptly disappeared. He was gone for four months before police finally brought him in on a warrant. Thereafter, the district attorney answered ready for trial within the six-month period required by the speedy trial statute.

Approximately twenty-two months passed between the People's announcement that they were ready for trial and the actual start of the trial. The trial judge found that this delay was caused "almost exclusively" by the defendant, who had requested and obtained the adjournments. The district attorney repeatedly stated his readiness for trial throughout this period.

Before the start of the trial, Jones's lawyer moved to dismiss the charges against his client on speedy trial grounds. He alleged that during the twenty-two-month period, the assistant district attorney took a planned European vacation lasting thirteen days. "These days should be charged to the state," he argued, "and that would bring them over the six-month mark and require the dismissal of charges against my client."

The trial judge denied the motion. Jones went to trial, was convicted, and was sentenced to four and a half to nine years. On appeal, Jones conceded that his guilt had been proved beyond a reasonable doubt. He claimed, however, that he had been denied a speedy trial.

The appellate court found that although the delays were mostly caused by Jones, there was the matter of the DA's thirteen-day vacation, which brought the People twelve days over the six-month limit. Jones was set free.

Look at the facts. Jones himself had sought and obtained extensive delays, but he refused to consent to the prosecutor's taking a vacation after he had answered ready for trial numerous times. It was this vacation that resulted in dismissal of the charges.

Such speedy trial statutes require neither a balancing of interests nor findings that the defendant had been prejudiced. As we see in the case of Jones, the defendant doesn't even have to demand a speedy trial, or be ready for a speedy trial, or even *want* a speedy trial in order to obtain the benefit of the statute. One would think that the failure of a defendant to show an interest in receiving a speedy trial would be considered a factor in weighing whether his rights have been protected.

Another defendant, Abraham Rodriguez, had charges dismissed because the prosecutor mistakenly relied upon the judge's erroneous calculations regarding the time by which the state would have to answer ready for trial. The defense attorney—no fool, he!—remained silent about the error at the time the judge made it. However, on the appointed date, when the prosecution answered ready for trial, the defense moved to dismiss all charges on speedy trial grounds. The court granted the motion and held that the defense was under no obligation to correct a miscalculation by the court and the prosecutor.

Once again, truth was sacrificed without any meaningful achievement of other values.

It is an illusion to believe that the endless intricacy of these statutes meaningfully relates to the problem of speedy trials. Reliance on mechanical formulations is part of the problem, not part of the solution.

These statutes are not really speedy trial statutes at all. They are prosecution readiness statutes. The only question is whether the prosecution is ready within the fixed time limits.

We do not ask: Is the defendant ready for a speedy trial? Does the defendant even *want* a speedy trial? If the DA is ready, will we have a speedy trial? If he is not ready, will the defendant be denied his right to a speedy trial? Burdened by the statutes, we quickly lose sight of the values that prompted our concern in the first place.

The amount of litigation produced by these statutes has been extraordinary. Almost every day, law journals contain lengthy opinions by trial judges that detail, following protracted hearings, whether a particular delay was "includable" or "excludable." An adjournment may only have taken a moment of the court's time but the inquiry regarding it can drag on and on, endlessly delaying the trial.

What if we were to set aside these arbitrary statutes and consider the real issues:

- What constitutes unreasonable delay?
- What are the true impediments to speedy trial?
- Do volume and complexity relate to the time frame in which a speedy trial might occur?
- Are there circumstances when a defendant waives his right to a speedy trial by virtue of his own lack of diligence?
- Is dismissal of charges the only viable sanction for speedy trial violations?

We should begin by canceling mandatory time periods in favor of evaluation on a case-by-case basis. Then, in order to show that the right to a speedy trial has been denied, we should require a defendant in a criminal case to demonstrate that he had at least some interest in a speedy trial in the first place.

| 6 |

THE THEATER OF THE ABSURD

Anything Goes in the
Modern American Courtroom

The more I see of lawyers, the more I like my dog.
MY MOTHER

The aspect of our criminal justice system that frustrates people the most is that it seems so rife with game playing. Too often, attorneys appear to be so involved with their own concerns that the issues of justice and fairness become secondary. Such behavior only encourages cynicism on the part of the public. And as an officer of the court, I have the unpleasant task of making sure that the games stay out of my courtroom. It's not always in my power to succeed—a lesson I learned once again from my experiences in the Pedro Gil case.

When I was assigned the case of the *People of the State of New York* v. *Pedro J. Gil,* I never imagined that I would become entangled with the most high profile case of our era. But it shouldn't have surprised me because in our current adversarial system, dramatic ploys and show-stopping tactics are par for the course.

It all started on the night of October 8, 1993, in Washington Heights, a bustling multiethnic neighborhood on the northern tip of Manhattan. That night, Pedro Gil, a Dominican busboy, was alleged to have thrown a thirty-pound bucket of spackling compound from the roof of a building, striking and killing Police Officer John Williamson.

Whenever a police officer dies in the line of duty, it generates a tremendous public outcry, and this case was no different. Although Gil initially fled to the Dominican Republic, he was eventually convinced by family members to return and face arrest.

Pedro Gil appeared in my court on May 25, along with his attorney, Peter Neufeld. Gil was a typical New York City defendant—one who lacks the resources to hire a private attorney and is either assigned a public defender or represented pro bono (free of charge) by a local attorney. In this case, Gil was being given the services of Peter Neufeld, an attorney who regularly did pro bono work.

During the pretrial conferences, Neufeld suggested that he would be presenting an active defense—that is, he would show some relevant circumstances that questioned Gil's liability. I set the trial date for September 28.

Then came June 12 and the murders, three thousand miles away, of Nicole Brown Simpson and Ronald Goldman. About two weeks before Pedro Gil's trial was scheduled to begin, Peter Neufeld arrived in my chambers, accompanied by Margaret Finerty, the prosecutor assigned to the case. Neufeld requested a two-month postponement. He told me he had been retained to handle the complex DNA hearings in the O. J. Simpson case. Neufeld assured me his role would be completed and he would be ready to try the Gil case in two months.

I questioned Neufeld carefully and told him that I was skeptical that two months was enough time. Already, the O. J. Simpson case had all the earmarks of a slow-motion train wreck. It seemed unlikely that the jury selection and DNA hearings would be wrapped up in two months. I didn't want to be in a position of granting Neufeld a two-month postponement only to have him return and ask for more time, so I recommended that he go ahead with Gil and join the Simpson trial in November.

Neufeld assured me that I was mistaken. He was certain that he would be done with his part in the Simpson case within two months. To prove his good faith, he added, "I give you my word as a man of honor that even if the Simpson hearings are *not* completed by November 28, I will go forward with Gil." Neufeld further stated that he really had no interest in participating in lengthy hearings out in Los Angeles. "I'm a family man," he told me sincerely. "If it looks like the DNA hearings are going to last more than three weeks, I wouldn't want to be away from my family that long."

I granted a postponement until November 28, and re-arranged my calendar.

By mid-November, I was beginning to get edgy. Along with everyone else in America, I saw the news reports of the Simpson hearings. The alternate jurors had not yet been selected and the DNA hearings hadn't even started.

Even so, I tried not to worry. Neufeld had given me his word. I felt Neufeld's associate, Barry Scheck, could handle the Simpson matter while Neufeld went ahead with the Gil case. But that wasn't what Neufeld had in mind. He wanted another postponement. I wasn't about to grant it, but Neufeld turned up the heat. One morning, I received a call from Judge Lance Ito, who was presiding over the Simpson trial.

"Do you know who I am?" he asked.

"Oh, yes, I know who you are," I said with a chuckle. I could also guess what he wanted. He told me he was calling at the request of Peter Neufeld. I explained why I would not consider another postponement.

I was tremendously frustrated and disgusted. My memory was crystal clear, even if Peter Neufeld's was not. He had given me his word as "a man of honor" that he would be ready November 28, and I was determined to go ahead with the trial. I wasn't trying to be a curmudgeon, and the last thing I wanted was to be drawn into the Simpson media frenzy. But in a court of law, everyone's rights are equal whether their legal tab runs in the millions or is pro bono. My job as a judge was to make absolutely certain of that. It would be a gross disregard of my ethical duty for me to make a decision that O. J. Simpson's trial took precedence over Pedro Gil's—a case that was now fourteen months old.

Long ago, I learned that the worst possible thing a judge can do is lose his temper in court. It solves nothing. It's undignified. And it only aggravates an already explosive situation. But I could not tolerate the disingenuous way Peter Neufeld tried to further delay Pedro Gil's trial, and as I entered the courtroom on November 28, I was fuming.

As I faced Neufeld, I was prepared to do battle. Neufeld was flanked by a team of lawyers to represent *him* against me, the wicked judge. They were a familiar cast of characters led by the flamboyant William Kunstler. I had known Kunstler most of my career, and tended to view his presence in a courtroom as an invitation to histrionics. I hoped I wouldn't have to deal with him. It was my intention to soothe some of the ruffles by outlining in a factual way my understanding of the chain of events.

"Just so we can have some background on this matter," I began, "the case of Pedro Gil grows out of an incident that occurred on October 8, 1993, a period almost fourteen months ago. The indictment in this matter was filed on November 4, 1993.

"Back on May 25 of this year," I continued, addressing my remarks to counsel, "we fixed a date certain for hearings and trial for September 28, 1994. Approximately two weeks earlier, Mr. Neufeld came into my chambers with Ms. Finerty to request a two-month adjournment. Now Mr. Neufeld seeks an additional adjournment.

"I have spoken to Judge Ito in California. He called me. And Judge Ito indicated that he does not expect to begin the DNA hearings until mid-January of next year. When Judge Ito asked me how I felt about Mr. Neufeld's application before him, I indicated that I thought his request of Judge Ito was outrageous in the circumstances." I could see the displeasure registered on Neufeld's face. Ignoring his reaction, I went on.

"Mr. Neufeld has maintained throughout that since he does not seek an acquittal for Mr. Gil—that he's only seeking a conviction of manslaughter in the second degree—and Mr. Gil will be sentenced to jail, that it's okay with Mr. Gil and Mr. Neufeld that this case be adjourned into the indefinite future."

I leaned forward in my chair and gave Neufeld a hard look. Speaking slowly for emphasis, I said, "It is *not* okay with the district attorney. It is *not* okay with me. And it is *not* okay with the deceased police officer's family who also have interests in these proceedings. Mr. Neufeld is not the center of *their* universe."

I issued my ruling to Neufeld. "You'll answer 'Ready' on December first, and we'll go forward or you'll answer, 'Not ready.' And I will hold you in contempt for not going forward, until such time as you are ready, and I'll put you in jail."

Neufeld immediately rose to protest. He denied ever making a firm promise to be ready for Gil regardless of the status of Simpson. "Unfortunately, your honor, I believe you are confused about what was said at that time," he insisted.

"I'm confused about you being a man of honor, too," I shot back.

Neufeld's face reddened. He started to interrupt, but I waved him to silence. I wanted to make my point absolutely clear. "The principle I'm trying to announce here, and finally without interruption, and what I've avoided saying until now," I said impatiently, "is that you came to me in September and said you were a DNA expert and this is a DNA expert's case of the century."

As Neufeld frowned at me, I paraphrased the words I remembered him speaking so clearly in our private conversation: " 'Judge, you've got to let me go. My fame and fortune rely on Simpson.' "

Neufeld nearly jumped out of his skin. "That's a lie, your honor!" He hopped from one foot to another gesticulating wildly. "That's a lie and you're doing it to distort the record and you should withdraw it. You're invoking your own personal bias to try to taint these proceedings . . . and you should be ashamed."

"Sit down." I was outraged, not because of the personal attack as much as the arrogance of the man. He really did believe the world revolved around him. He seemed completely insensitive to the injustice of his position. And now he was attacking me to cover up his own misbehavior.

"Your honor," Neufeld cried, "I'll tell you why it's a lie."

"Sit down," I ordered again. "Just sit down. This proceeding is now concluded. You're losing your temper."

But he wouldn't stop. Finally, I ordered the court officer to put him in jail until he cooled down. That had an immediate effect of quieting him, at least for the moment. I adjourned court and went to my chambers. During the next few hours, I was hounded by members of the press who smelled blood and wanted a piece of the action. This was just the kind of incident the press savors.

What bothered me most about this whole sorry affair was that it was played in the press as a David and Goliath story. Poor Peter Neufeld. Torn between two judges. What was he to do? I felt that public sympathy would be on his side, but to me the issue was clear. Neufeld was like a performer con-tracted for a bit part in an off-off Broadway play who sud-denly gets offered the lead in the biggest hit on Broadway. His dilemma was not caused by me; it was of his own mak-ing. He wasn't at all the hapless victim of arbitrary justice that he portrayed himself to be. For one thing, I had repeat-edly given him the option to withdraw from the Pedro Gil case and allow another attorney to be appointed, and he refused. No, he said, I want to try this case. It's not as though he were trapped without a choice or free will.

In an irony that was not lost on regular court observers in this time of judicial madness, the case was about the *lawyers,* not about their clients. In a bizarre twist of fate, it seemed that the population of competent attorneys had been reduced to a handful—all of whom were engaged in representing O. J. Simpson. In the process, Neufeld had made himself (and, consequently, Simpson) the center of the system. The family of a dead police officer in New York City didn't mat-ter to him. Nor did the court's calendar. Nor did the rights of Pedro Gil and the state of New York.

Regrettably, that's the point we've reached in our practice of the law. Honor, fidelity, fairness, and duty are replaced by the interests of fame, fortune, and public spectacle.

Regardless of my personal feelings, I could not stop Neufeld from appealing to the appellate court, which ultimately ruled in my favor. The trial of Pedro Gil proceeded, but it felt like a hollow victory. The whole public show seemed so much smoke and mirrors. Incidentally, Neufeld's showboating was irrelevant, as it turned out. The Simpson lawyers waived pretrial DNA hearings, and Neufeld didn't even appear in court until April 1995. None of this had to happen, but sadly, it was a sign of the times.

During the long months that the O. J. Simpson trial wound on, people often asked me if this was normal. To the average viewer, the display often seemed more like madness than law. Indeed, presiding over my own courtroom, I sometimes feel as if I am the ringmaster in some gladiatorial arena. Theatrics, not truth, is the guiding principle. Strength is the ultimate test.

At a trial, we have two gladiators in the ring—the defense and the prosecution. The defense lawyer's only goal is to represent his client. His only interest is his client—not society, not the victim. This man, the defendant, is entitled to a champion who will say on his behalf everything that can be said in the hopes that through such a challenge we can be satisfied that the resulting product will be one that has integrity.

In a court of law, only the prosecution is assigned the task of seeking the truth. Since we know that truth is not the sole or even the primary objective, we give the side that's not seeking the truth ample opportunity to suppress the truth within the law.

How does that alter the relationship between the two sides? The prosecutor says, "I believe this man is guilty and I'm going to seek his conviction."

Given that, it's up to the defense attorney to decide how he wants to proceed. It's not always easy, because often defendants say they're innocent no matter how great the evidence against them.

It's a strength-testing process. The defense strategy has nothing to do with the truth. It has to do with the odds.

Sadly, the culture that the defense lawyer inhabits today is one that says it's okay to push the envelope, to brush against the ethical barrier and occasionally slip over. The temptation to be overzealous can be very great. Statistically, about 90 percent of the people who go to trial in this country are guilty. That puts defense lawyers in a situation where they're constantly representing guilty people. That's how the envelope gets pushed. That's where the line gets crossed between pure zeal and the excessive zeal that is designed to confuse, cloud, or hide the truth.

On the other hand, the prosecutor's life is a constant call to accountability. Every time a prosecutor makes a mistake and the defendant is convicted, the case may be called up on appeal. Too often, the appellate court, the arbiter of courtroom rules, reverses convictions based on a small mistake or a technical error. That's accountability!

The popular notion is that it's the prosecution's job to get a conviction, no matter what. But that has not been my experience. I remember an occasion when the head of the Trial Bureau, Nancy Ryan, came to see me in my chambers. She was preparing to try a case that seemed strong, and since she's a talented lawyer, she had a good chance of getting a conviction. But Nancy was disturbed.

"Quite frankly, Judge, I've got problems with this case," she told me.

"How so?"

"Well," she said, "it's a one-witness identification and that troubles me. You know, Judge, one witness comes in and says this is so, and I challenge her and I question her and I test her and she gives me the right answers. But I've got a feeling up my spine. There's something off about this case."

This was certainly an interesting turn of events! "So, what does your office do in that kind of a situation?" I asked Nancy.

"We have a policy that if one DA feels uncomfortable about prosecuting a case because the person may not be guilty, the case is reassigned to another DA. And if the other DA investigates it and feels the same way, the case will be dismissed. Even if it seems there's sufficient evidence to take to a jury. And if the other DA investigates it and feels it's a good case, the other DA will prosecute."

I was impressed with Nancy's honesty as well as with her integrity. It confirmed my faith in the way cases are prosecuted.

Although the defense and prosecution are considered enemies to the death in this gladiator ring we call the courtroom, it has almost always been my experience that prosecutors do not want to risk sending an innocent person to jail.

Nonetheless, it's not surprising that our current system of criminal justice would breed cynicism, since so much of the time it seems focused on everything but truth-seeking.

Viewed one way, from the very instant police officers place a citizen under arrest, that citizen embarks on a journey, aided and abetted by the Constitution of the United States, that was exquisitely designed to impede or prevent the truth from ever seeing the light of day. The reason for these protections is clear. But I wonder: Have we diminished the value of truth to the extent that it no longer matters?

In the past thirty-five years, our courts have focused intently on the need for fairness; both sides in a criminal case must be free to contend vigorously for vindication, and must be assured of a fair and full hearing. But our adversarial system in its attention to fairness has spawned excesses—most notably, an excessive tolerance of efforts by the contestants to distort the truth.

In 1980, Marvin Frankel, then a federal district judge, wrote in a short book, *Partisan Justice,* that the "search for truth" in the courtroom "fails too much of the time." Frankel maintained that "our adversary system rates truth too low among the values that institutions of justice are meant to serve."

Is Frankel correct? If a trial is not a search for truth, what is its point? Is it not ultimately a waste of our time and our resources? These are deep and complex questions, but I assure you they are not abstract. There are few things more meaningful and more firmly rooted in our community life than the way the state interacts with its citizens—especially when that interaction is the result of a crime against the community.

Increasingly, I suspect that the real issue is *not* one of ethics but of structure. The way our adversarial system presently works not only *diminishes* the possibility of truth, it *encourages* and fosters excess on the part of the lawyers vying for the upper hand. The goal has become victory, not truth. Our courtrooms have become casinos, with a professional culture of misconduct so pervasive and so profound that it is often unrecognizable as justice. Because we have ceased to see it clearly, we have also ceased to question it honestly and rigorously.

There has been a lot of talk inspired by the O. J. Simpson case that perhaps police and prosecutors sometimes "rush to judgment"—conspire to bring a person to trial without having proper evidence. That has not been my experience. Indeed, it is a ludicrous proposition. If it is true that volume is the dominant existential reality of the criminal justice system, why would prosecutors undertake to charge persons whom they did not believe were probably guilty and then assume the burden of proving the charges?

Our entire system prior to a defendant going to trial is composed of a set of probability screens. Defendants don't just show up in court on a whim, railroaded by the system. By the time a person reaches trial, he has been deemed "probably guilty" several times—by the grand jury and by the court in preliminary hearings. It might shock your notion of justice to hear me say that the majority of defendants are "probably guilty." But if you think about it, you'll realize that that's preferable to saying that most of the people we arrest and bring to trial are "probably *not* guilty."

You might wonder, though, how we can presume a defendant is innocent when we say he is probably guilty. First of all, the presumption of innocence is a *trial* presumption—it does not relate to the earlier stages of the process. It is a way of stating that the burden of proof is on the People, not the accused; it is a way of telling the jury to keep an open mind, don't jump to conclusions prematurely and don't presume he's guilty because he's in the courtroom. It's a way of saying to the jury: "Be fair. The People have accused this man. Now, let's see if they can prove it." Note that *no one* pleads innocent, and no one is found innocent. Defense attorneys don't argue innocence, they argue reasonable doubt. (The average defense attorney might say that a trial is not a search for truth but a search for reasonable doubt.)

What the presumption of innocence does *not* mean is that the defendant is probably innocent. If that were the case, there would be no righteous grounds to make an arrest. It would be a police state where "probably innocent" citizens were arrested arbitrarily. Unless there existed some grounds for regarding a person legally guilty, it would be morally monstrous to bring a charge against him, indict and jail him, and compel him to undergo the ordeal and disgrace of a trial.

The best way to put it is this: The trial is the process by which we go from a reasonable probability or warranted suspicion of guilt supported by evidence to an assertion under law of legal innocence or guilt.

Since most defendants are in fact guilty of some or all of the charges, the usual defendant on trial is yearning neither for an accurate reconstruction of the facts nor for an error-free trial. (That is not to question the standards of presumption of innocence or proof beyond a reasonable doubt; although most defendants are guilty, not all are, and we don't know in advance who is and who is not.) So, the defense attorney resists, demands, opposes, and objects more than the prosecution, and is more often overruled. With the intention of being overruled, a defense attorney will often seek to "seed the record" with error. Issues will be raised for no other purpose than to provoke error.

It is only a short step from seeding the record with error to judge baiting. Although our professional ethics would seem to forbid such behavior, there is no bright line between acceptable courtroom gamesmanship and misbehavior. And the defense attorney's guild has never publicly condemned the view, as Marvin Frankel puts it, that "A judge is, in season and in due measure, fair game." A victory gained by provoking judicial blunders is a victory all the same.

Although a judge is committed to the search for the truth, he is also required by the rules of the game to sit helplessly by while professionals are engaged in a clearly deliberate and entirely proper effort to frustrate the search.

Yet it is the judge, ultimately, who must control the courtroom, rein in the lawyers, and instill a sense of dignity and sobriety to the process. I truly believe that judges get the lawyers they deserve.

Five years ago, a colleague of mine did a study in which she put people in different courts throughout the city to determine how different judges processed felons. She had the occasion to watch the same lawyer before ten different judges. He was a different lawyer each time, depending on the standards a particular judge held him to. Judges control the courtroom—either by action or omission. They have a big responsibility.

But the lawyers have a responsibility, too. They can argue the issue before the judge, and the judge then has to decide it. It's simple—as long as the judge maintains authority. It shouldn't even be a problem because, like any other gamesmen, these gladiators truly want clear rules. I think they have a yearning for rules, for order, for discipline. But if the judge doesn't control the process, they'll fall out of line.

I had a funny incident some years ago with a lawyer, now deceased, named Joe D. Joe was what we called a Baxter Street lawyer. He practiced out of a little storefront behind the courthouse. And he looked the part—porcine and kind of greasy, with a slick toupee perched ceremoniously on top of his head. Now, Baxter Street lawyers aren't exactly the cream of the profession, but Joe was very bright and very realistic. He saw things clearly, and there was no nonsense about him. He did a good, workmanlike job.

One day Joe walked into my courtroom, prepared to do a voir dire, which is the questioning of prospective jurors. He was wearing a garish tie—a bright pattern of orange and lime green. It was a truly ugly tie. It could make you cringe, that tie. It fell halfway over his substantial belly, hanging like a whorehouse flag.

The first thing Joe did when he stood up to address the prospective jurors was to grab his tie and push it forward into their faces, booming, "See this tie? See this tie? How many of you don't like this tie?"

"Joe," I chastened him at sidebar, "in my view, that is not a proper question. It demeans the process. It makes it silly. It makes it like a circus. Whether that is your intent or not, it is not an appropriate question on voir dire. If you think people are not going to like your tie, wear a tie that you think they will like. If you have no questions on voir dire don't ask any. But this is not a proper question."

Joe responded very candidly. "Judge," he said, "you say it's not a proper question. I've been doing this for twenty years. I've appeared in every courtroom in this building and no other judge has ever stopped me. And you know why they don't stop me, Judge? Not because you're wrong. You're not wrong; you're absolutely right. They don't stop me because that's my only goddamn question. Okay? And they're so happy to have a short voir dire that they let me ask anything. Okay? Now, if that's not okay, I don't have any other questions. But don't blame me. Every judge in this building lets me do it except you."

I had to laugh. In his direct way, Joe told it like it was. And, of course, his purpose in asking about the tie was clear. He knew he wasn't Robert Redford. He wanted to get a feel for the way the jury responded to him. His intention wasn't so bad. But my view was, and is, that dignity must prevail in the courtroom.

Dignity is something that has been left by the wayside in the street-fight atmosphere of our modern courtrooms. I wouldn't mind seeing it come back. I recently mentioned to a friend that I wished American lawyers would wear robes, as English lawyers do. He laughed at the idea—until I suggested he consider the circus of the O. J. Simpson trial. "Maybe there would be less personality in lawyering and more aware- ness of limits," I said. "That would be a fine thing. In my courtroom, I want more sonnets and less blank verse. Let the creativity and genius of lawyers express itself within limits. Our lawyers are too self-involved."

The movie *Anatomy of a Murder* epitomizes the specter of excessive zeal. In the film, James Stewart plays the defense attorney and George C. Scott plays the district attorney. We know the "good guy" is Stewart from the very beginning— even though he does all the bad things.

The defendant, played by Ben Gazzara, walks into a crowded bar and shoots the bartender five times, killing him. When Stewart goes to meet him for the first time, he doesn't ask, "What happened?" Rather, he tells Gazzara not to say anything, that he will talk for a few minutes and then go for coffee while Gazzara thinks about what he's said. He then goes on to describe to his client the various possible defenses that might be used. He could choose the defense of misiden- tification—although the bar was filled with people who saw him do the shooting. Or, he could use the defense of self-defense—although the bartender was unarmed and Gazzara initiated the incident. Or, he could use the insanity defense—that he didn't know what he was doing.

Stewart tells Gazzara to think about his options while he goes for coffee. When Stewart returns, Gazzara tells him he hadn't known what he was doing. The insanity defense it is! Stewart has, in effect, suggested the defense, and attorneys do this all the time. And in the course of the trial, Stewart (supposedly in the name of justice) throws evidentiary documents across the courtroom, threatens to punch out the DA, yells at witnesses, and says whatever he pleases.

If this were only a movie, we might laugh and shrug it off. But it is more than a movie. The public expects high drama in the courtroom, and lawyers are too often excused when they engage in it. In the last state trial of mob boss John Gotti, flamboyant defense attorney Bruce Cutler did *exactly* the same things—down to shouting, "Hot dog!" and "Touchdown!" when he got an answer that he liked.

There are many places we can look for a cure to the out-of-control adversary system. But perhaps the best place to start is with a serious reevaluation of the role of the defense attorney.

The role of the defense attorney is to zealously represent his client within the bounds of the law, to defend his client whether he is guilty or not guilty, and so to attack the accusing witnesses whatever the truth of those accusations may be.

But can we conceive—and *should* we conceive—of a system in which defense attorneys would be more willing to view themselves as part of a system of law, and less willing to see themselves as the alter ego of their client?

Society has conferred on the legal profession a monopoly over the rendition of legal services, and has delegated to it the power of self-regulation in the belief that lawyer domination and lawyer centrality in the trial process will best serve the public interest—yet that belief and that assumption has not been justified in the event.

Still, it is fair to ask whether the system serves the public interest.

In 1966, Professor Monroe Freedman, a leading ethics scholar, asked what he described as "The Three Hardest Questions" (of a criminal defense attorney):

1. Is it proper to cross-examine for the purpose of discrediting the reliability or credibility of an adverse witness whom you *know* to be telling the truth?
2. Is it proper to put a witness (including the defendant) on the stand when you *know* he will commit perjury?
3. Is it proper to give your client legal advice when you have reason to believe that the knowledge you give him will tempt him to commit perjury?

Professor Freedman answered all three questions in the *affirmative*—and thereby launched a storm of controversy that has yet to settle.

In twenty-five years on the bench, during which I have handled literally thousands of criminal cases, I have *never* been approached by a defense attorney plagued by *any* of these conundrums.

These are, unfortunately, everyday practices of the criminal defense lawyer. Freedman's questions were answered with ease and comfort a long time ago. And because they grow out of the confidentiality of the attorney-client privilege, they never reach visibility within the system. Only academicians—not courts—deal with these "hard" questions today.

We have never resolved the issue of the proper balance between zealous representation and the obligation of the lawyer to the court and to the public.

We may condemn the histrionics of lawyers as simply the tawdry business of amoralists doing what they find tolerable to earn a living. But this willingness to perform adversary stunts runs deeper than greed. It interferes with the very nature of the process.

The defense attorney cannot be just a "mouthpiece," but neither is he a public servant. He must be permitted and obliged to assert the rights that are available to his client under law.

Given the probability that the defendant is guilty, the defense attorney knows that the defendant will win *only* if counsel is successful in *preventing* the truth from being disclosed—or, failing that, misleading the jury once it is disclosed. So, when the defendant is guilty, the defense attorney's role is to prevent, distort, and mislead.

Our professional ethics and our procedural law are intertwined. Much of what appears at first to be an ethical question is actually a question about the wisdom of our rules of evidence and procedure, and the better course may often be to change the procedural rule.

Thoughtful people have disagreed about the objectives of the adversarial system. But when a practice is defended solely on the ground that it is necessary to support the system, it is fair to ask whether it will further the good of the system.

Lawyers simply are not the appropriate persons to correct the defects of the adversarial system. Their hearts will never be in it, and it is unfair to both their clients and themselves to require them to serve two masters. We must take action on a judicial level to right the wrongs that neither side in the adversary system is capable of righting.

| 7 |

THE PLEA BARGAIN

Tortured Outcome of
an Overwhelmed System

Not long ago, a woman came before me on a charge of grand larceny. She was a bookkeeper who was accused of stealing from her company by writing checks to herself, which she then cashed. Her attorney told me that she disputed the charge, saying the checks she cashed were salary checks.

Well, right away her contention seemed improbable. In my experience, bosses don't ordinarily have employees arrested for cashing their paychecks. But there was other evidence, as well—including the endorsed and canceled checks, written in amounts that were greater than her salary, as well as the fact that she had pulled the same stunt in her previous job. She had a prior felony conviction for the same kind of conduct.

Like all defendants, this woman had the right to a trial. But it was fairly likely that she would be found guilty. When the DA offered a plea that was less than she could normally expect to get, her attorney persuaded her to go with it. She had everything to gain and nothing to lose.

Plea bargains, which require the defendant to plead guilty to at least some of the charges, are close to a truth-finding process. Certainly, that was the case with this woman.

Plea bargaining has been a dominant factor of our system since the Warren Court revolution, which established a multitude of procedures and protections for accused persons. The main reason for its dominance is the system's volume and complexity. We'll never again have a system that's so simple that plea bargaining won't be necessary. Today, anywhere from 90 to 95 percent of all cases are plea-bargained. And like it or not, there is no escape from it. So, the question is, How do you plea bargain and what should your principles be? How should you go about doing it in a way that protects society?

Let me emphasize how dominant the factors of volume and complexity are to any understanding of the criminal justice system. The volume problem is perhaps not as well understood. Let me give you an example. In Manhattan, in the mid-1990s, we have 125,000 cases that come through our arraignment court each year. How do we dispose of those 125,000 cases? Ultimately, the cases lead to between 12,000 and 14,000 indictments. Those are the serious cases that are sent to the New York State Supreme Court. The remainder of 111,000 to 113,000 cases are misdemeanors, violations, and lesser charges. These are handled in the criminal court.

How are we set up to process that kind of a volume? In the criminal court, which deals with misdemeanors, we have ten trial parts. If each trial part worked at maximum efficiency (which it doesn't), it would try two cases per week. That would total 20 cases, times 50 weeks, or about 1,000 cases a year. In fact, because things don't work optimally, the most cases that have ever been tried in any single year in criminal court has been 350.

Now, take the supreme court. The New York State Supreme Court has a total of 40 trial parts. Because felonies are more complex, we'd hope to try one case a week, for a total of 2,000 cases a year. In fact, we've never been able to try more than 1,000 cases in supreme court in any given year. So you have a maximum trial capacity of about 1,350 cases a year. And since there are approximately 2,500 cases coming in each week, our annual trial capacity is less than a week's worth of cases.

So we go to plea bargaining out of necessity, not out of desire. It is inescapable. Now, the difference between the two courts is also significant. If you have about a thousand trials in supreme court, that's about 10 percent trial capacity. In criminal court, however, the percentage is closer to 1 percent. Basically, criminal court has become a paper-pushing process. It has effectively ceased to be a court at all.

In December 1963, when Henry C. Alford was indicted for first-degree murder, his attorney questioned all but one of the

witnesses before the trial who the defendant said would substantiate his claim of innocence. The witnesses, however, did
not support Alford's assertion of innocence, but instead gave
statements that strongly indicated that he had committed the
murder. The trial court, prior to acceptance of the defendant's plea of guilt, also heard the sworn testimony of a police
officer who summarized the state's case.

Although there were no eyewitnesses to the crime, the testimony showed that shortly before the killing the defendant
took his gun, said he was going to kill the victim, and then
returned home and said he had done so.

Faced with strong evidence of guilt and no substantive evidence for his client's claim of innocence, the attorney recommended that he plead guilty and try to work out the best deal
he could with the DA. "It's up to you," he told Alford, "but
I think you should do it."

Alford said that he was not guilty, but he would plead guilty
because he faced the threat of the death penalty if he went to
trial, and he reasonably believed he would be found guilty if he
went to trial. (North Carolina still had the death penalty in
1963.)

The prosecutor agreed to accept a plea of guilty to a charge
of second-degree murder, and eight days after he was indicted, Alford pled guilty to the reduced charge—although he
continued to protest his innocence. After the trial court
elicited information regarding Alford's prior criminal record,
which was a long one (he had previously served six years of
a ten-year sentence on a *prior* murder, had been convicted
nine times for armed robbery, and had also been convicted of

transporting stolen goods, forgery, and carrying a concealed weapon), the trial court sentenced Alford to thirty years, the maximum for murder two.

On appeal, Alford claimed that his plea of guilty was invalid because it was the product of fear and coercion.

In 1968, the Court of Appeals for the Fourth Circuit *reversed* Alford's conviction on the grounds that his plea of guilty was made involuntarily. It held that the court encouraged the defendant to waive constitutional rights by the promise of no more than life imprisonment if a plea of guilty was accepted, and that the plea of guilty was involuntary because its principal motivation was fear of the death penalty.

The U.S. Supreme Court, however, reversed the court of appeals and *upheld* the defendant's plea of guilty. The Court stated that the standard should be whether the plea represents a voluntary and intelligent choice among the alternative courses of action open to the defendant. That Alford would not have pleaded except to eliminate the death penalty did not necessarily demonstrate that the plea of guilty was not the product of a free and rational choice. The trial court had made independent inquiry and satisfied itself that the defendant's belief that he would be convicted of murder one was justified and rational.

The Court further stated that since guilt, or the degree of guilt, is at times uncertain and elusive, a defendant, though believing in his innocence, might reasonably conclude that a jury would find him guilty and that he would fare better by a plea of guilty. The defendant must be permitted to judge for himself in this respect. So while most pleas of guilty consist of both a waiver of trial and an express admission of guilt, the latter is *not* constitutionally required. Here, the evidence substantially negated the defendant's claim of innocence and the trial court was satisfied that the plea of guilty was intelligently entered.

One of the concerns about plea bargaining is that it is unfair and coercive. In fact, in a famous article, Professor John Langbein, a well-known legal historian, actually sought to draw parallels between plea bargaining and the medieval European law of torture. His thesis was that there were striking similarities in origin, in function, and even in specific points of doctrine between the law of torture and the law of plea bargaining.

Although I strongly disagree with some of the conclusions Langbein draws about plea bargaining, I do agree that the parallels between torture and plea bargaining "expose some important truths about how criminal justice systems respond when their trial procedures fall into deep disorder."

From the mid-thirteenth century to the mid-eighteenth century, a system of judicial torture lay at the heart of Continental criminal procedure. The application of torture was a routine and judicially supervised feature of European crime procedure. Under certain circumstances the law permitted the criminal courts to employ physical coercion against suspected criminals to induce them to confess.

The law of proof in the thirteenth century required that a conviction had to be based on the testimony of two unimpeachable witnesses to the crime. Only if the accused voluntarily confessed could he be convicted without the eyewitness testimony. But it became clear that the standard of proof was set too high. Clearly, some crimes were not committed within view of anyone.

To quote Langbein, "Because society cannot long tolerate a legal system that lacks the capacity to convict unrepentant persons who commit clandestine crimes, something had to be done to extend the system to those cases. The two-eyewitness rule was hard to compromise or evade, but the confession rule seemed to invite the 'subterfuge' that in fact resulted." The criminal justice system moved from accepting a voluntary confession to coercing a confession from someone against whom there was a strong suspicion. The law regulating torture was designed to deal with this process of generating confessions. The European judges also devised a rule of probable cause so that only persons highly likely to be guilty would be examined under torture.

In order to comply with the requirement that a confession be voluntary, a confession that was obtained under torture was treated as involuntary unless the defendant repeated it free from torture at a hearing a day or so later. However, a defendant who confessed under torture, recanted, and then was tortured anew soon learned that only a "voluntary" confession at the hearing would save him from further suffering.

Because torture tests the capacity of the defendant to endure pain rather than his veracity, and because the innocent might yield to the torment, the system was basically flawed as a way of ascertaining truth.

According to Langbein, the parallels between plea bargaining and the system of judicial torture are "many and chilling." Langbein's basic contention is that each of these substitute procedural systems arose in response to a breakdown in the formal system of trial.

The American system of justice, burdened by volume and complexity, and incapable of functioning according to its mandate, makes it very costly for a defendant to go to trial by threatening a materially increased punishment if he does so. This sentencing differential, Langbein argues, is what makes plea bargaining coercive.

Of course, the torture victim was coerced into a confession that condemned him to the severest punishments, whereas the plea bargain *rewards* the defendant with a *lesser* sanction.

No one likes the necessity of plea bargaining. It is a simple fact that plea bargaining sacrifices those values that the unworkable system of adversary jury trial is meant to serve: lay participation in criminal adjudication, proof beyond a reasonable doubt by the prosecutor, the right to confront and cross-examine witnesses, and the privilege against self-incrimination.

Let's examine the criticisms that plea bargaining is essentially coercive and unreliable—nothing more than a modern-day version of the rack. More often, the absolute opposite is true; criminals get less than they deserve, not more.

I had a case earlier this year in which a woman came before me who was a lifetime shoplifter. The charge was that she stole $5,000 worth of merchandise from Macy's. I saw by her record that she had sixty-three previous shoplifting arrests. Some of them were grand larcenies that had been reduced to misdemeanors. In those cases, the prosecutor actually undercharged because he lacked the resources to charge a woman who steals more than a thousand dollars from Macy's with grand larceny. He needed to use his limited resources for the murderers, rapists, burglars, and so on. It's pretty common for felonies to be undercharged in this way. Grand larceny auto is treated as a misdemeanor. Grand larceny for large amounts of shoplifting and so on also gets reduced to a misdemeanor. It's a matter of priorities. The volume and the complexity of the system require the prosecutor to concentrate resources on those cases that most seriously threaten the public good.

In effect, what we've done with the persistent shoplifter is to de facto legitimize shoplifting. This woman expected to be charged with a misdemeanor and take her thirty days in jail as the cost of doing business. But the day she landed in my court was not her lucky day, because now she was told she was facing a felony.

And she said to me with a true sense of indignation, "Judge, I've been doing this for ten years already, and I've never been charged with a felony." She couldn't accept that she might be facing four years in state prison for this, her sixty-fourth arrest.

As I listened to her, it dawned on me that this woman felt that a felony charge was a breach of promise. On sixty-three prior occasions, she'd been arrested and gone to jail for thirty to sixty days. But now we were changing the rules and she was looking at four years. It wasn't fair!

She couldn't understand what had happened, and I didn't really blame her. For years, we had been telling her that she could shoplift with very little consequence. Burdened by the volume and complexity of our cases, we had given her a license to steal.

But when she learned she was charged with a felony, she didn't want to plea, even though the evidence against her was overwhelming. She went to trial, was convicted, and I sentenced her to seven years. The offer of four was no longer open. When I gave her seven years, she looked at me as if she hadn't heard right. "Did you say seven *months*?"

"No, seven *years*."

So, on the one hand, when we talk about the criminal court, plea bargaining has effectively decriminalized many minor offenses because we just don't have the capacity to process them. What we have is what one commentator calls a Cadillac system in which we give some people, like O. J. Simpson, only the finest legal treatment. He had many lawyers; he got immediate attention; and the case moved to trial within ninety days. Ten percent of felons get this kind of Cadillac treatment. The other 90 percent do not. We offer them protections only as a way of permitting them to exercise leverage on the system. We say to them, The only thing you can bring to this system is your capacity to burden it.

To put it bluntly, a defendant can either take up the court's time and expense, or he can save the court's resources by accepting a plea.

There is a separate concern that plea bargaining is too lenient—that, basically, it's a revolving door. There's some truth to that. Why would a defendant who is guilty plead guilty unless you offered him less than he would otherwise get?

Here's a case that illustrates the argument about plea bargaining. Paul Lewis Hayes was a petty thief in Fayette County, Kentucky, who passed bad checks. He'd been arrested a number of times and received several felony convictions. So he was a persistent felony offender.

He was arrested again for passing a bad check in the amount of $88.30. Ordinarily, this crime was punishable by two to ten years in prison. Before trial, the DA offered him five years for a plea of guilty. The DA also warned Hayes that if he went to trial and was convicted, he would seek a ruling under the Kentucky Habitual Criminal Act, which carried a mandatory sentence of life imprisonment.

Hayes refused to take the plea. He went to trial, was convicted, and was sentenced to life. He then appealed to the U.S. Supreme Court on the grounds that he was being punished for exercising his right to a trial.

The U.S. Supreme Court denied the claim, explaining that the DA had no obligation to plea-bargain. The DA offered a plea bargain with a sentence that was relatively minor; the defendant had a choice of taking it or going to trial; the defendant was informed in advance of trial what the consequences would be if he was convicted; and he still chose a trial.

The Court noted that "The open acknowledgment of this previously clandestine practice has led this court to recognize the importance of counsel during plea negotiations, the need for a public record indicating that a plea was knowingly and voluntarily made, and the requirement that a prosecutor's plea bargaining promise must be kept."

Very often, I'm confronted in my courtroom with a situation where a defendant comes before me and I have some extraneous considerations to deal with. Are the witnesses available? Are there courts available? I have two murder cases that are waiting. I don't want to use that part for a burglary case when I have a murder case. There are all kinds of factors weighing upon me that have nothing to do with what this defendant deserves.

And I'm ready to tell this defendant he doesn't deserve a lenient sentence. I might say, "I'm prepared to give you one to three years instead of three to nine years, not because you deserve it but because I have other things I have to do that require my attention more than you do. So I will give you a sentence that is below what you should get. Of course, if you go to trial and you're convicted, I won't punish you, because that was your choice. But I will give you what you deserve."

It's tricky. I try to look at the true issues. What am I really doing? That's a fair question. Am I punishing him for going to trial or am I punishing him by giving him his just deserts without regard to the extraneous factors that I previously had to consider?

Now, almost always, you'll find that the defendant who goes to trial gets sentenced more severely if he's convicted than the defendant who pleads guilty. So the claim is that we're coercing him into pleading guilty.

It isn't always the case that a plea results in a more lenient sentence. Some years ago, I had a truly horrendous murder case, and I had to decide what was right.

This case involved an elderly Puerto Rican man who had come to New York only about ten years earlier. He and his wife had raised two sons in Puerto Rico, and after his sons had grown up and left home, they took in a young, homeless orphan girl and began to raise her. After his wife died, the defendant followed his sons to New York and brought with him the orphan girl, who was now fifteen and whom he treated as a daughter. With his very modest pension, they lived together on the Lower East Side in a small apartment.

The young girl started to go out with a handsome lout who soon got her pregnant. She gave birth to a baby girl, but remained at home with the defendant, who continued to care for her and the child. By all accounts the defendant adored the baby, who was his only grandchild.

The young girl's lover never contributed anything to the support of the child or his paramour, but each weekend he would come by and take the young mother to his apartment, leaving the defendant to take care of the baby. The defendant came to resent the lover, but held his tongue.

After some months of this, there came a Sunday afternoon when the defendant was in his apartment with some elderly friends, playing cards and drinking. The lover came by to drop off the young mother.

The defendant was a little high. He asked the man, "Why don't you bring some milk or diapers for the child?" The lover said, "It's my job to fuck your daughter, and your job to support the child."

This enraged the normally calm defendant. He reached into a nearby drawer and withdrew a loaded pistol, which he pointed at the lover and fired. Tragically, he missed the lover but hit his granddaughter in the head, killing her instantly.

When the case came to court, the elderly man was offered a plea bargain of only eight years in prison, since there were clearly mitigating circumstances. He didn't take it, but went to trial, where he was convicted of manslaughter. I ended up giving him less than eight years because once I'd heard all the evidence and listened to the witnesses, I found the poor man more sympathetic than before the plea bargain. In this case, going to trial worked to his advantage.

But I had another case some years ago that worked the opposite way. L.R. was a corrupt businessman who, in company with others, had stolen something like $150 million. Many famous stars were defrauded—Eddie Murphy, Kirstie Alley, Cliff Robertson—and many sophisticated and professional investors as well as many small and unsophisticated persons were duped. L.R. wasn't the mastermind, but I would say he was number three in the organization and he had a significant role. All of his colleagues pled out, but L.R. wanted a trial.

This was destined to be a long trial—maybe three months. There was lots of paper and many, many witnesses. The DA's office didn't want to use its scarce resources taking L.R. to trial, so he was offered a plea bargain of one to three years, which was a very generous offer. He refused, so we had a long trial and L.R. was convicted.

During the course of the trial, I got to see L.R. on a daily basis. I heard all the witnesses come forth to describe how they were defrauded and how they lost their businesses and their homes. Some of the stories were heartbreaking.

After L.R. was convicted, I sentenced him to sixteen to forty-eight years, which was at that time the longest white-collar crime sentence in New York, and it was upheld on appeal. The sentence was based on what he deserved for his criminal acts—free of all the extraneous considerations that the district attorney and the court had to contend with prior to the trial.

My view is that plea bargaining is ethically neutral—there is nothing about the way it should operate that is intrinsically wrong. Like any human system it has those who abuse it. Neither I nor the judges I know use it punitively. When a defendant is convicted after trial, the question that is asked is: What is the proper sentence for this defendant? *Not,* How should this defendant be punished for going to trial?

What *is* wrong with plea bargaining is that because of volume and complexity we are often required to offer a defendant a *discount*—an *inducement*—to plea bargain. This discount is a sentence *less* than the defendant deserves and should receive (although one that, hopefully, bears some relationship to his criminal act). We do this in order to achieve promptness, certainty, and finality of result—all of which are otherwise lacking in our system.

Now, of course, every defendant *must* choose whether to plea bargain or go to trial, and some perceive the need to choose as coercion, but this is absurd. Every aspect of our daily lives requires us to make choices. If the defendant is well informed about the choices he must make, and he has counsel, and the proceeding is open and on the record and aboveboard, then the choice he makes is not coerced—any more than my choice to be a lawyer rather than a doctor was coerced.

So, we are compelled to make choices, but the choice the individual makes is not coerced by the state.

The choice is almost always dictated by the strength of the People's case—by the defendant's judgment that he is likely to be convicted and that he is likely to do more time when he is convicted after trial. Indeed, it is the *state* that is coerced into plea bargaining, *not* the defendant. The defendant wants the leniency that plea bargaining offers, and he seeks it— indeed, he comes to rely on it.

Let's examine the criticisms of plea bargaining one by one. Perhaps the leading critic is Professor Albert Alschuler of the University of Chicago School of Law. Alschuler has identified the following problems, but I think you'll agree that most of the arguments don't hold up to scrutiny.

- Plea bargaining makes a substantial part of an offender's sentence depend not upon what he did or his personal characteristics, but upon a tactical decision irrelevant to any proper objective of criminal proceedings.

It may be true that extraneous factors play a role in the agreement arrived at, but the seriousness of the charge, the strength of the case, and the defendant's criminal history are factored in when plea bargaining occurs. Obviously, plea bargaining can be done well or badly—as can trials.

- In contested cases, plea bargaining substitutes a regime of *split the difference* for a judicial determination of guilt or innocence, thus avoiding the requirement that criminal responsibility be established beyond a reasonable doubt.

In a sense, this argument *contradicts* the claim that plea bargaining is coercive, that the defendant has no choice. Here, both sides carefully calculate their strengths and weaknesses and arrive at a consensus that must then be approved by a judge.

- Plea bargaining deprecates the value of human liberty and the purposes of the criminal sanction by treating these things as commodities to be traded for economic savings.

It is human nature to try and bring leverage to a situation and to seek what is in one's best interest. That is all that is occurring here.

- Plea bargaining leads lawyers to view themselves as judges and administrators rather than as advocates.

An advocate, in order to be effective, must see things clearly and objectively, and assess the strengths and weaknesses of his client's position. What is wrong with that if, in his client's interest, he reviews all of the defendant's options?

- Plea bargaining subjects lawyers to serious financial and other temptations to disregard their client's interests, and diminishes confidence in the attorney-client relationship.

It is illusory to believe that the unethical plea-bargaining lawyer is an ethical trial lawyer; that the lazy and uninformed plea-bargaining lawyer is an energetic and well-prepared trial lawyer. That certainly has not been my experience. A good lawyer is a good lawyer and plea bargaining has nothing to do with it.

- Plea bargaining is inconsistent with the principle that a decent society should want to hear what an accused person might say in his defense.

At first blush this seems more like an attack on the Fifth Amendment than on plea bargaining, for even at trial we may not hear what a defendant has to say, and we may not even draw inferences from his silence. Indeed, in plea bargaining, the defendant *does* say he is guilty and the reduced plea may reflect the appropriate mitigation. We may actually hear as much or more from a defendant who plea-bargains as one who goes to trial.

- Plea bargaining undercuts the goals of legal doctrines as diverse as the Fourth Amendment exclusionary rule, the insanity defense, right of confrontation, and the defendant's right to attend criminal proceedings.

This is hyperbole, and reaching. Obviously, the defendant attends the court proceedings whether he pleads guilty or goes to trial. Obviously, if he is guilty he may not wish to confront those he has victimized. As for the insanity defense, it is *always* a last ditch, in extremis, defense, *never* raised except when the evidence of guilt is overwhelming. And the argument that plea bargaining undercuts the exclusionary rule is ridiculous because, as we have already seen, the law of search and seizure is largely unknowable and almost impossible to legislate. It is a wild card; neither side knows whether they will win, so they compromise in a plea bargain.

- Plea bargaining almost certainly increases the number of innocent defendants who are convicted.

The argument here is that even an innocent man may plea-bargain if the proffered sentence is low enough and the danger of an enhanced sentence after trial is present. But this is true *only* if there is a reasonable possibility that the defendant will be convicted at trial. The People must prove guilt beyond a reasonable doubt, and the operative screens have already found the defendant to be probably guilty. So only an innocent defendant, who has been found probably guilty and who perceives a reasonable likelihood that he may at trial be found guilty beyond a reasonable doubt, will be so tempted.

When I was a defense attorney, I would often have defendants who protested their innocence in cases where the proof of their guilt was literally overwhelming. I indicated to those defendants that the likelihood that they would be convicted at trial was great and that it might be better to be an "innocent" man doing two years instead of an innocent man doing ten years. They almost all agreed—to their benefit if not society's. For these defendants, innocence was a pose, a stance they took perhaps because they could not accept responsibility for their conduct. Or, perhaps, they thought their attorney would work harder for them if they proclaimed their innocence.

But there were also cases where the proof was not, in my view, overwhelming, where the case was triable and there was a reasonable possibility of acquittal. That also meant that there was a reasonable possibility of conviction. However, a jury trial is a crapshoot. No one knows how good the witnesses will be on the stand or whether the jury will credit their testimony. In this situation some innocent defendants may plead guilty where, without plea bargaining, they would go to trial.

But are we certain, in this kind of situation, that a fairer or more just result would be obtained by a jury trial? Is the jury infused with some wisdom that the experienced and knowledgeable attorneys on each side are lacking? In any event, what is so terrible about offering the defendant in this situation a choice?

As common as plea bargaining is, the fact remains that not everyone is eligible. There are times when you don't want to give a discount, where you can't realistically give a discount. I had a case last year in which there were three defendants who were engaged in a series of abhorrent crimes. It was alleged that these men followed women home, then pushed their way into their apartments. If there were people at home, they tied them up, then ransacked the apartments and raped the women—often in front of their families.

The case against the three men was very strong. Should I give them a discount for pleading out?

Not really.

I told the defendants, "Your offer here is twenty-five to fifty years." One man took the offer. The other two went to trial, were convicted, and were sentenced to five hundred years each.

Since plea bargaining is designed to help the court prioritize, it's not relevant for the truly horrible cases. Some years ago, I had such a case. The defendant was driving a big roller tractor, the kind that smoothes out wet asphalt on pavement. He had been smoking marijuana. And under the influence of marijuana, he was piloting a two-hundred-ton tractor; he never saw the car parked in front of him. He rolled right over the car, crushing a woman and her two children. He kept right on riding, not even aware of what he'd done.

By the time he was arrested, about twelve hours later, the marijuana in his system had metabolized and only traces were found. It looked like a very weak case.

The DA came to me and said, "Judge, he's ready to take a manslaughter plea if you give him probation."

I shook my head. "I'm not going to give him probation. I'd rather that you try the case and lose than send him out on probation. He killed three people while he was under the influence of marijuana. If he's guilty, he ought to go away for a long time. If I let him go it demeans and distorts the whole process. A mother and two children are dead. If he walks out on probation, what we're doing ceases to have any meaning."

In order for plea bargaining to be meaningful, there has to be a relationship between the seriousness of the charge, the strength of the charge, and the sentence that is imposed. If you don't properly evaluate those factors, there's no point to the exercise.

In the Baz case (the shooting of Hasidim on the Brooklyn Bridge, which I discuss in the next chapter), the defense attorney was very interested in entering into a plea bargain. But the charge was so serious and the evidence so strong, that I said I could not offer anything less than thirty-five years to life. The defense attorney said that was no inducement. It wasn't—and it wasn't intended to be. Plea bargaining permitted that case to go to trial within six months of the event. Plea bargaining permits us to prioritize.

The fact that justice is a strength-testing process never becomes clearer than in the area of plea bargaining. Let me give you an example of that.

Let's say you have identical twin brothers, same exact background, same prior criminal record, same school, same parents, same everything. And they're walking down the street and in front of them are two women. Brother A decides he's going to rob Woman X and Brother B decides he's going to rob Woman Y. So A runs up and robs one woman and B runs up and robs the other woman. They've done exactly the same thing in exactly the same way. Justice would seem to suggest that they be treated exactly the same way.

However, let's imagine that Victim X was Jane Smith, the dean of the Columbia University Law School. And Victim Y is Joanie Schmoe, who is a drug addict and prostitute, just in from California on her way to Florida. Jane Smith is going to be a terrific witness. Joanie Schmoe will be gone with the wind. She won't stick around for the trial.

Those two cases have got to be treated differently. Brother A, who robbed Jane Smith, faces ten years. No doubt about it. Brother B, however, has a less certain destiny. Since his victim will probably not show up to testify against him, chances are he'll get a chance to take a plea for ninety days. It's a very real world that plea bargaining deals with.

I am reminded of an incident that occurred when I was a young Legal Aid lawyer in the early 1960s. I was assigned to a criminal court part that was being presided over by the newly appointed administrator, Judge John Murtagh, who had a tough, severe reputation and who despised plea bargaining.

The part had a calendar of about a hundred cases a day and Legal Aid handled about 80 percent of those, so it was a very heavy load. On the first day Murtagh called me up to the bench and said, "There will be no plea bargaining in my courtroom."

I told the judge respectfully but firmly, "If there is no plea bargaining, there will be no pleas."

He frowned down at me from the bench. "We'll see about that," he said.

True to my word, there were no pleas that day, and no pleas that week. The caseload backlog grew by four hundred that week.

The following Monday, Judge Murtagh called me in and said there would be plea bargaining after all. Right or wrong, the reality of volume made it so.

The simple fact is this: There is no alternative to plea bargaining in our system. If your goal is to end plea bargaining, you must infinitely expand the resources available to the system—or you must change the system.

No one really likes plea bargaining. But until our legislatures choose to put more money into our courts, and until we find ways to operate them more efficiently, and until we agree that many of our laws are creating more problems than they solve, plea bargaining will remain a necessary fixture.

| 8 |

POKER-FACED JUSTICE

How Liberal Discovery Laws Can Hide the Facts
and Subvert the Truth

> The adversarial system of trial is . . . not yet a poker
> game in which players enjoy an absolute right always
> to conceal their cards until played.
> BYRON WHITE,
> U.S. Supreme Court

When the trial of Rashid Baz was assigned to my courtroom,
I knew it would be a complex and volatile situation. This was
a wildly emotional case, capable of reaching inflammable
proportions because it involved the murder and attempted
murder of a group of Hasidic students by a troubled Lebanese man.

From the moment the news first hit the airwaves, it
appeared that this was a brutal attack without any provoca-
tion. A van full of Lubavitch Hasidic students was returning

to Brooklyn after a vigil at the Manhattan hospital where Rabbi Menachem Schneerson had gone for treatment. Rabbi Schneerson was the elderly spiritual leader of the Lubavitch community. Some believed he was the Messiah. Although his hospitalization was for a relatively minor procedure (he later fell into a coma and died the following year), there had been a continuous vigil of followers outside the hospital.

As the van carried the students across the Brooklyn Bridge, a car sped into view. Pulling alongside the driver's side, a man in the car began firing a machine gun into the van. The van careened wildly, flinging its screaming passengers from their seats. When it came to a stop, one student lay dead, another gravely injured. Other students stumbled out of the van, stunned and suffering slight injuries.

The car sped away, leaving the scene of death and destruction, and police began the process of investigation. A lucky tip from a garage worker to whom Baz brought his car was the break in the case. Rashid Baz was arrested.

It's easy to imagine that the public execution of a Hasidic youth by a Lebanese man would create a huge stir in New York. At first, many suspected a terrorist plot, but as the evidence was compiled, it appeared that Baz acted alone. I was relieved that the Arab community decried Baz's action. It lessened the possibility that the trial would turn into a circus, with Arabs and Jews forming hostile groups in the courtroom.

Baz's attorney, Eric Sears, was a good lawyer with a tough sell. He had to convince a jury that his client did not knowingly fire two machine guns at a van filled with Hasidic students crossing the Brooklyn Bridge, that he did not knowingly kill one, severely injure another, and mildly injure several others.

Sears began by examining the People's case, as he was entitled and obliged to do under the discovery statute. Discovery provides the defendant with a complete overview of the People's case without requiring from him, in any form, his own version.

But every defendant *has* a version, and it should not depend on what the People say happened.

Invariably, when a defendant has not yet committed himself to a story, the defense he chooses tracks the weakest aspect of the People's case. This occurred with Rashid Baz. When he was first arrested, Baz proclaimed his innocence. He said, "I don't know what you're talking about. It wasn't me."

Then, as he learned of the evidence against him, Baz altered his position. "It was me," he admitted, "but I did it in self-defense. Men in the van were firing at me."

At last, when it became clear that self-defense wouldn't wash, since no guns were found in the van, Baz changed his story yet again. Now he claimed that because of his mental state, he "believed" he saw men firing at him. In effect, he was not aware of what was really happening.

That's the journey Sears and Baz took to reach the decision to plead insanity. Given the overwhelming evidence against Baz, Sears couldn't present a defense that his client wasn't there and didn't do it. He had in his possession a mountain of prosecution documents and tapes that forcefully made the case. So, Sears had to consider his client's position from every angle—and he had to play for time. By law, Sears had to give advance notice that he would be relying on an insanity defense. But he delayed providing the notice until after discovery and until he was sure he could find "experts" to support the defense.

Finally, Sears announced that Baz's defense would be insanity. A psychiatrist would testify that Baz suffered from a condition called Post-traumatic Middle East Stress Syndrome (which court observers later dubbed "PT-Mess"). The syndrome, Sears said, stemmed from Baz's youth in war-torn Lebanon. As a result of the traumas in his childhood, he was unable to judge reality. Therefore, when he said people in the van were firing at him, he really believed they were.

Naturally, the prosecution requested a report to substantiate the claim. After all, Middle East Stress Syndrome was a brand-new defense, never argued before. When no report was forthcoming, the prosecution complained to me. I asked Sears about the psychiatrist's report.

"We have no report," Sears replied.

"How about the notes the psychiatrist took when he interviewed Baz?" I asked.

"He didn't take notes," Sears replied.

Now, if you're a logical person, you're going to think that's strange. The psychiatrist interviewed Baz and he didn't take any notes? He formulated an entire psychological opinion—even went so far as to elaborate upon a new clinical condition, Middle East Stress Syndrome—and he didn't write anything down?

This is part of the game. Defense attorneys typically tell experts not to take notes in order to avoid having to turn them over. But imagine the district attorney trying to use this same gambit, claiming that police didn't take notes. No one would believe it. To the contrary, in the course of its investigation, the prosecution had generated an enormous amount of discoverable material. When an arrest is made, the cops write reports every step of the way. Each time a witness is interviewed, a report is made. In the Baz case, that meant hundreds of pages of documents. Even the most insignificant point was notated. And yet Baz's lawyer, with a straight face, said in court, "Your honor, the psychiatrist who examined my client did not take any notes."

You may find this disingenuous, but that's the way the game is played. It's a symptom of the morass we've created with the discovery statute. The prosecution must turn over every scrap of evidence, but the defense can find a dozen ways to get out of providing anything at all. Furthermore, when the prosecution turns over its evidence, it too often magically becomes the basis for the defendant's case.

Many years ago, as a defense attorney, I was assigned a case where the defendant was charged with forcible rape. I played the discovery game just the way every defense attorney worth his salt does.

During the rape, the victim's father returned home. When he entered the apartment, the rapist fled through a window. He was caught about half an hour later several blocks away.

The victim claimed she had been asleep in her bed and woke to find the defendant, a complete stranger, on top of her. When I first interviewed the defendant, he claimed that the act was consensual, that he had met the young girl earlier in the day and she had invited him home after they had walked and talked in a nearby park. The defendant argued that the girl was now crying rape out of shame and embarrassment because her father had caught them in the act. "She said she was afraid of him," my client told me.

I was prepared to believe my client until I received the state's discovery material. There, as plain as day, was the information that would make a lie of my client's story. According to the material, the girl and her father had arrived in the United States only a few weeks earlier—from what was then Yugoslavia—and neither of them spoke a word of English.

When I learned this, I realized that my client's story was not plausible. She didn't walk and talk with him in the park. She couldn't have. She didn't speak English. I confronted my client with these newly discovered facts. He then admitted that he'd lied to me. "Here's the truth," he said. "I've never seen the girl before."

"Why did you tell me you had a relationship with her?" I asked.

He shrugged. "It sounded more believable."

So the defense became mistaken identity.

It was my right—indeed, my responsibility—as a defense attorney to do this. There is no secret about this process. Robert Shapiro, in the O. J. Simpson case, blatantly stated for all to hear: "We'll devise a defense once we know what the state has to offer." A vivid example of the way the defense shaped its case around discovery occurred at the very beginning of the trial during opening arguments.

Simpson's story to the police had been that he was sleeping inside the house, which is why he didn't hear the buzzer when the limousine driver arrived to take him to the airport. But once the defense reviewed the prosecution's case, they discovered that there were two problems with this story. One was that the limo driver reported seeing a large man hurrying across the lawn toward the house shortly before the interior lights went on and Simpson responded to the buzzer. The second problem was that cellular phone records showed that Simpson had made several calls on his car phone during the period in question.

In his opening arguments, Johnnie Cochran abandoned the sleeping O. J. story and suggested that his client was actually outside in the yard chipping golf balls at the time. This would account for his presence in the yard, and for his decision to make phone calls from the car instead of returning to the house. While the new story might have seemed a bit thin, it was a logical strategy since all the defense had to do was plant a reasonable doubt in the mind of one juror.

The case of the Menendez brothers is an even more powerful example of the discovery game. In the beginning, Lyle and Eric Menendez denied killing their parents. Only when it became apparent that the evidence of their guilt was overwhelming did they devise the self-defense/child abuse story that became the centerpiece of the trial. It's notable that not a hint of this defense was mentioned in the years prior to the case coming to trial. Throughout the investigation, the boys continued to proclaim their innocence. Only when the defense received discovery materials, including a taped confession one of the boys had given to a psychiatrist, did the story change. What followed was a surprise defense, seemingly concocted at the last minute, that told a sordid tale of years of sexual abuse at the hands of an evil father, culminating in the night when Lyle and Eric became convinced their parents were planning to murder them. Enough members of the jury bought the story for a hung jury to result. At this writing, the Menendez brothers have just started their second trial. One wonders if the "surprise" defense will work a second time.

I see it all the time in my courtroom. Defense attorneys regularly take unfair advantage of liberal discovery guidelines to manipulate the system.

At the beginning of a trial, I always tell the prosecution and the defense, "Give me the names of all of your witnesses or your potential witnesses. I want to read their names to the jurors so I can find out whether any of the jurors know any of the witnesses. We don't want jurors who know witnesses." More often than not, no witness list comes from the defense.

Then, when the prosecution finishes its case, the defense attorney may say (with the jury out of the room), "Your honor, I have two witnesses out in the hall. I want to call them."

I'll be annoyed. "What do you mean you have two witnesses you want to call?" I'll demand. "You told me you had no witnesses."

The attorney will grin sheepishly. "Yes, well, I just discovered these witnesses."

I know this is often untrue, but what do I do? Do I keep the witnesses out? No. However, I don't appreciate the tactic. It doesn't have much to do with justice, the law, or finding out the truth.

Like many other rules governing criminal trials, the discovery statutes are relatively new, and they vary widely from state to state. Thirty-five years ago, defendants were entitled to little if any discovery; it was believed that the prosecution was not obliged to potentially weaken its case by showing its hand in advance. In 1953, discovery became one of the most heated battles in jurisprudence with the case of the *State of New Jersey* v. *Tune.*

On October 7, 1952, the grand jury of Essex County, New Jersey, returned an indictment charging John Henry Tune with the murder of William Prather. The body was found in the decedent's basement, and Tune was arrested that same day. During a five-hour interrogation by police, Tune admitted to the murder and signed a fourteen-page confession. The trial court, in its discretion, allowed Tune and his attorney to inspect the confession before the trial, but denied him the right to inspect the statements of others. On appeal, the Supreme Court of New Jersey reversed the ruling that Tune was entitled to read his own statement, and affirmed the decision that he needn't have been allowed to read other statements, thus denying all discovery.

By a narrow majority, the court ruled that the accused was not entitled to a copy of his confession. The decision, written by Chief Justice Arthur Vanderbilt, centered around the belief that discovery led not to greater fact finding and pursuit of truth but to just the opposite—a tendency to perjury and falsification. In effect, the majority held that a defendant who knows exactly what the prosecution's case entails can then concoct a story that fits the facts. For instance, a defendant who claims he wasn't at the scene might scurry to develop a plausible story for why his hat was left there. (As my mother said, "If he can rob, he can lie.")

Vanderbilt held that "long experience" had taught that liberal discovery in criminal cases would "lead not to honest fact finding, but on the contrary to perjury and suppression of evidence"—and that discovery concerning witnesses would facilitate bribery and intimidation and would deter witnesses from coming forward.

Because Vanderbilt believed that the Constitution would not permit reciprocal discovery, he felt that one-way discovery would "make a prosecutor's task almost insurmountable."

In a heated dissent, Justice William Brennan (who would later be appointed to the U.S. Supreme Court) blasted Vanderbilt's reasoning. "Few issues raise more sharply the basic ideological clash between opposed theories of criminal justice," he wrote.

Brennan pointed out, reasonably enough, that discovery was a necessary component of fairness. A trial, he said, should not be a sporting contest. The defense has a right to be prepared, to know what evidence the prosecution will present against its client. However, his position that liberal discovery would further the search for truth and make a trial less of a sporting contest ignored the ways the defense would play this high-stakes poker game.

Chief Justice Vanderbilt did not dispute the need for fairness. But, he wondered, wasn't there a possibility that a person accused of a crime, especially if that person were facing prison, might use that information to invent a more convenient story? Might not someone who was desperate for a way out go so far as to *lie* about the facts? Vanderbilt was concerned about giving information to people who had a vested interest in lying.

Both men were right. Yes, an accused person has the right to hear the evidence against him. And yes, it is not outside the bounds of imagination that he might then use that information to formulate his defense—even lie to save his skin. But, as you know, our legal system is not fond of ambivalence; you can't say that both points are right. You have to choose one. And the trend since *Tune* has been toward much broader discovery. There are several reasons for this.

Of primary concern is the basic notion of fairness to the defendant. But in this context, the meaning of fairness stems from the criminal justice system's primary goal of determining truth. And that goal is impeded when pretrial preparation is hampered by a lack of information.

Another argument for broad discovery is that it promotes guilty pleas (thus expediting cases), and it promotes early identification of trial issues, causing fewer delays and interruptions. These considerations, however, reflect lofty ideals that are far removed from reality. They assume, for one thing, that defendants will be as eager to seek a just and efficient resolution as the DA. That's simply ludicrous. It's more likely that defendants will use witness statements to fabricate a consistent defense and destroy the People's case.

It is ironic that while the philosophy behind the *Tune* decision has lost much of its force when it comes to prosecutorial disclosure to the defense, it still thrives when the issue is defense disclosure to the prosecution.

The defense lawyer's only goal is to represent his client with zeal, within the bounds of law. He's not interested in society. He's not interested in the victim. His client, the defendant, is entitled to a champion. And his lawyer will perform that function in every way possible within the limits of the law.

However, the specter of misuse is there. Sadly, witness intimidation is a reality I have seen in my own courtroom. And I am mindful of a New York case involving a gang of assassins called The Vigilantes. When two members were charged with murder, the district attorney argued against turning over the name of the witness to the defense. He told the judge there was a real concern about the safety of the witness. The judge, abiding by the strict rules of discovery, denied the prosecution's request. The name of the witness was given to the defense the day before the trial was to begin. That night, the witness was murdered.

We cannot deny that witness intimidation takes place. We can wish it weren't so, but it's an unfortunate result of trying to get "bad guys" off the street. Unfortunately, the problem of witness intimidation is growing worse, and the state is budgeting for more witness protection programs.

To be sure, the burden of proof in a criminal case is on the state. The defense doesn't have to prove anything. And that's as it should be. But that doesn't really clarify the issue of discovery.

The irony is that discovery is not even constitutionally mandated except in a very limited way. The U.S. Supreme Court has held that the prosecution must turn over to the defense anything in its possession that is *exculpatory*—that is, any material that might support the innocence of the defendant. That's certainly fair. If the prosecution is charging you with a crime, but they have evidence that it might have been committed by someone else, it would be a gross injustice not to require them to disclose that evidence. But according to the Constitution, the prosecution doesn't have to turn over anything else.

Every state in the union has a statute that controls and orders discovery, and these statutes vary widely. That's one reason a trial becomes a lottery; depending on where you live, there might be a very strict or very liberal discovery statute.

Even in states where reciprocal discovery is required, the balance is not equalized. Since the Fifth Amendment protects defendants from compulsory self-incrimination, as a practical matter, reciprocal discovery does not meaningfully exist.

In liberal disclosure states, discovery received by the defense is virtually an open file, while discovery received by the prosecution is limited to information the defense intends to use at trial. The way the law rests at this point, it is questionable whether there is a constitutional basis for any state to go beyond that.

The bottom line is that no defendant is required to disclose the fruits of his investigation to the DA. If the defense finds inculpatory witnesses—that is, witnesses who would incriminate the defendant—or if he conducts scientific tests, they need not be disclosed if he does not intend to use them. For example, O. J. Simpson's lawyers conducted their own DNA tests, but the results of these tests were never presented. Why not? Because they were too incriminating. Meanwhile, the defense was able to plant suspicion and doubt about the results of the prosecution's tests, never revealing that their own laboratory may have come up with the same result.

Arguably, a system committed to truth would not permit one side to hide information that is relevant to the truth-seeking process. Truth may be the paramount goal but it conflicts with other values—here, the need for procedural fairness and a respect for human dignity and limitations on government power.

The hard question is: Does the concept of fairness in criminal procedure transcend the concern for truth?

As Professor Grano has pointed out, say a rule does not increase the risk of wrongful conviction, violate the defendant's dignity, or permit abhorrent governmental behavior. In this case, it is hard to know in what sense the rule can be considered unfair. Nevertheless, the claim is frequently made that certain rules are unfair simply because they make the conviction of a defendant more likely. Defense attorneys argue that discovery from the defense is unfair, even if constitutional, because it eases the DA's burden of proving guilt.

But such discovery does not increase the risk of *erroneous* conviction, intrude upon human dignity, or permit governmental misconduct, so the assertion of unfairness in this context seems to mask an indefensible claim that facilitating the discovery of truth is unfair.

It's that old familiar theme. The belief that the prosecution's task should be made difficult for its own sake is based on the view that a criminal trial is like a sporting contest in which we are indifferent about the outcome. Such indifference is hardly appropriate in the administration of justice. If a defendant is guilty, he should be convicted. If he is not guilty, he should be acquitted. An erroneous acquittal should be a source of dismay, not indifference.

It seems to me there's a tendency toward pro-defense bias in the way we treat the matter of discovery in the courtroom. While we are very quick to preclude the DA's use of highly relevant and probative evidence, the exact opposite is true when the issue is preclusion of the defendant's evidence.

Consider the discovery violation of the O. J. Simpson defense in not disclosing a tape recording of an interview conducted with Rosa Lopez. Lopez, you will remember, was a maid employed by neighbors of O. J. Simpson. She was prepared to testify that on the night of the murders she was walking the dog and saw O. J.'s Bronco parked on the street—allegedly during the time he was said to have been committing the murders.

The California discovery statute requires the defense to turn over a list of witnesses, along with all relevant notes, tape recordings, and materials, yet the defense failed to notify the prosecution that there was a tape recording of an investigator's interview with Rosa Lopez. When the prosecution challenged the defense about the existence of tape recordings and reports made by an investigator, defense attorneys Carl Douglas and Johnnie Cochran clearly and unequivocally stated to the court that no tape recording of either of Lopez's statements was in the possession of the defense. The late disclosure resulted in a four-day delay of proceedings before the jury.

In considering the appropriate sanction for the delay of the disclosure of both the tape recording and second report, Judge Ito noted that Lopez was an important witness because her testimony conflicted with the prosecution's theory that the defendant used the Bronco to travel to and from the crime scene. Ito's sanction amounted to little more than a hand slap. He fined Cochran and Douglas $950 each.

Contrast that sanction with a later sanction imposed on the prosecution. When it was revealed that an important report related to Bronco fibers found at the crime scene had not been shown to the defense, Ito ruled that the information would be excluded altogether—even though it was, in his own words, "compelling circumstantial evidence."

Why was the sanction against the defense violation a small fine, while the sanction against the prosecution was exclusion of reliable evidence? One reason might be the fear of reversible error. A judge can't be reversed on appeal if he rules against the prosecution. Whatever the reasoning, a sanction that prevents good evidence from coming before the jury is not furthering a search for the truth.

An interesting case recently came before the New York Court of Appeals. The defendant, Rafael Flores, was accused of a despicable act: raping a six-year-old boy who lived in his apartment complex. Flores was brought to trial, and both the boy and his mother testified. Flores was convicted of four counts of sodomy in the first degree.

After the verdict but before sentencing, a police officer's memo book, which contained a single page of notes, was discovered and delivered to the defense. Now, under New York law, this single piece of paper could topple the whole house of cards. The judge, Lawrence Tonetti, however, took a different view. When the document in question was presented, he asked the defense attorney, "Did the failure to receive this document during the trial cause you any injury or prejudice?"

Flores's attorney studied the page of notes. In a rare and surprising moment of candor, he replied, "There is absolutely nothing in the memo book that would have made a difference."

In light of this, the judge let the conviction stand.

The case went to the court of appeals. The defendant claimed that his attorney had been an ineffective counsel because the judge would have been required to reverse the conviction and order a new trial if he had protested on the grounds of a discovery violation.

The court of appeals determined that this was not a case of ineffective assistance of counsel. There was no basis to disagree with the defense attorney's conclusion, and he should not be deemed incompetent merely because he did not pursue a frivolous claim as the basis for a new trial. Two judges (and, I'm certain, the entire defense bar!) dissented.

Every once in a while, common sense prevails. But only rarely.

What's the answer? Let's begin with a premise: If truth is the goal—and it is where discovery is concerned—there is no reason in law, morality, or common sense why a defendant's access to the People's case should not be conditioned on his willingness to give up any right to misuse that evidence. Therefore, from a policy perspective, the argument against full reciprocal discovery is hard to understand. Surprise, from either the prosecution *or* the defense, supports the idea that justice is a game of chance and wit, not a search for the truth.

If we believe that truth is the goal, I suggest a very simple solution. It's so simple, so obvious, so full of common sense, it seems unthinkable that such a plan would ever be adopted in a system as cluttered as ours. But perhaps this idea will see the light of day in the future.

I call it the Sealed Envelope Proposal. The Sealed Envelope Proposal provides a method that would both preserve the defendant's right to discovery and at the same time prevent him from using discovery material to concoct a false story.

After a defendant is formally charged with a crime, if he wishes to obtain discovery of the People's case, he should be required to write down his version of what happened and place the account in a sealed envelope. The envelope would then be turned over to the judge. The contents of the envelope would not be seen by the prosecutor or anyone else *unless* the defendant took the stand and testified in his own defense. Only then could the envelope's contents be revealed to assure that the defendant's story is consistent with his trial testimony or, in the event that it is not, it would be available to impeach him.

Since there is no constitutional right to discovery, the state is free to condition the terms under which discovery will be provided. Thus the Sealed Envelope Proposal.

We are not requiring or compelling the defendant to do anything. We are conditioning his access to the People's case on his assurance—in a sealed envelope—that he will not misuse the information for perjurious purposes.

In my opinion, being asked to place his story in a sealed envelope does not violate a defendant's rights. It does not convict the innocent. It merely prevents the lie.

| 9 |

SPEAK NO EVIL

The Truth, a Defendant's Accountability, and the Fifth Amendment

Sometimes silence is not golden—just yellow.
ANONYMOUS

Joel Steinberg did not take the stand to testify in his own defense. That was his right, even though he was the only person alive who witnessed the events that took place in the room where his daughter, Lisa, lost consciousness hours before her death.

The Joel Steinberg trial made headlines in New York. Even in a city that was accustomed to all manner of brutality, the fate of little Lisa Steinberg touched a raw nerve of outrage. When the case was assigned to my courtroom, I had to fight to maintain judicial objectivity. Every so often, a defendant comes before me who is alleged to have committed a terrible act, yet his face and demeanor betray no hint of conscience. Joel Steinberg was such a defendant. Day after day, he sat in stony silence at the defense table, his face a mask of aggrievement and quiet rage as witness after witness rose to testify.

The evidence against Steinberg was compelling. It showed that in the early evening of the night in question, Steinberg was at his Greenwich Village apartment with his six-year-old daughter, Lisa, his infant son, and his common law wife, Hedda Nussbaum. He had gone into the bedroom to dress for a dinner appointment he had with a "business associate."

Lisa asked her mother, "Can I go out to dinner with Daddy?"

"Ask him yourself," Hedda replied. Lisa went into the bedroom where her father was dressing. Soon after, Hedda would later testify, she heard a loud noise, and then Steinberg came out of the room carrying the unconscious body of his daughter. He laid her down on the floor of the bathroom and told Hedda, "Don't call a doctor. I'll heal her when I return." He then left the apartment and did not return for three hours.

To understand why Hedda Nussbaum did not call a doctor, even as her daughter lay unconscious on the floor, one must understand the Draconian environment that existed behind closed doors in the Steinberg apartment. On the outside, Steinberg was a cool and relatively successful lawyer, but his home was for many years a torture pit. Hedda would later show the court and the world the devastating bruises inflicted on her by Steinberg whenever she challenged his will. In seven days on the witness stand Hedda described incomprehensible scenes of violence and control, which culminated in Lisa's death. She tried to explain how it was that she did not seek help for her daughter in the hours after Steinberg left the apartment. He told her not to, and that was enough.

When Steinberg returned that night, he promised Hedda he would minister to Lisa after the couple freebased cocaine. But high on drugs, they paid no further attention to the stricken girl until six o'clock the following morning. By then, Lisa had stopped breathing. Failing to revive her, they called 911. When the EMS arrived, Steinberg told them Lisa's breathing trouble was from an attack she'd had trying to digest Chinese vegetables.

From the moment Steinberg was arrested for the murder, he maintained his innocence. In the courtroom, he sat glowering at witnesses, shaking his head, and fixing them with his "evil eye." But he never rose to testify in his own defense.

It was his right to remain silent throughout the trial. We do not require defendants to testify. But I found myself thinking that it was somewhat absurd that Steinberg would never take the stand. If his defense had been that he was in Europe at the time Lisa was killed and knew nothing about the circumstances, it would be understandable that he couldn't testify about what went on in the room that night. But he admitted that he was in the room. Lisa went into that room, and when he brought Lisa out she was dead—or near dead. There were facts about what went on in that room that only Joel Steinberg could relate.

Steinberg's rights were fully protected. He had a proper trial, and for two months he sat next to his attorneys and listened to all the evidence against him. Why shouldn't society have a right to subject this man—the one who admittedly was in the room with the young girl prior to her death—to an orderly procedure in open court where there would be no danger of his rights being trampled?

And what galled me most was that by law I had to tell the jury it could draw no adverse inferences from Steinberg's failure to testify, even though adverse inferences were perfectly logical and warranted under the circumstances.

There's a collapse of common sense here. Imagine this happening to you. Your husband goes into a room with your daughter, and when he comes out, she's unconscious. You ask, "What happened in there?" If he refuses to answer, wouldn't you draw an inference that he was behaving abnormally and that perhaps he had something to do with your daughter's condition? Of course you would! And so might any jury, except that I had to instruct them otherwise.

The instruction to the jury is a result of our interpretation of the Fifth Amendment right against compulsory self-incrimination. But the Fifth Amendment does not say that one might not draw reasonable inferences from the silence of a defendant. It merely states "No person . . . shall be compelled in any criminal case to be a witness against himself." At first blush, this would not seem to even remotely address the situation where a defendant does not become a witness.

It didn't seem right that Steinberg was not required to testify, at least to the facts as he knew them. But what enraged me was that after he was convicted, he tried to use the sentencing hearing as a soapbox for his defense. Since Steinberg was convicted of first-degree manslaughter, I had a great deal of latitude in sentencing. The sentence could be as light as two to six years or as heavy as eight and a third to twenty-five years. Faced with that, Steinberg suddenly wanted to talk. He wanted to tell his side of the story—to convince me of what his silence did not convince the jury, that he was innocent.

Steinberg began to speak. In long, rambling sentences he explained that it had all been a terrible mistake. He was a good father. "Lisa was well nourished, happy, healthy," Steinberg told me. He argued that the bruises on her body had not been caused by him but were the result of rough treatment by the emergency medical team. He went on and on, and I listened politely but with growing disgust.

"Mr. Steinberg, you are beginning to repeat yourself somewhat," I said finally, putting an end to the monologue. He sat down and I proceeded to sentence him to the maximum. Steinberg had waited too long to tell his side of the story. The Fifth Amendment may have protected him from that necessity during the trial, but it was too late now.

Prior to 1965, the U.S. Supreme Court was relatively clear on this matter. In 1947, in *Adamson* v. *California,* the Court stated: "It seems quite natural that when a defendant has opportunity to deny or explain facts and determines not to do so, the prosecution should bring out the strength of the evidence by commenting upon the defendant's failure to explain or deny it . . . the facts may be such as are necessarily in the knowledge of the accused. In that case a failure to explain would point to an inability to explain."

That changed in 1965 with *Griffin* v. *California.*

In *Griffin,* the defendant was convicted of murder in the first degree. Griffin chose not to testify at his trial, and in conformity with the California constitution, the DA argued to the jury that a person accused of a crime in a public forum would ordinarily deny or explain the evidence against him if he truthfully could do so. Also in accordance with California law, the judge instructed the jury that it was the constitutional right of a defendant that he may not be compelled to testify. But the jury could take the failure of the defendant to explain himself into account when rendering its verdict.

In the appeal of Griffin's conviction, the Supreme Court had to determine whether the defendant was "compelled . . . to be a witness against himself."

Clearly, Griffin had not been compelled to testify. He had not, in fact, testified. Nevertheless, the issue of compulsion was the focus of the Supreme Court's inquiry, even though it was a very different scenario than the specter of force that gave rise to this protection in the first place.

In the dark past, when a suspect was brought before the Star Chamber (essentially a torture chamber), he was *commanded* to answer questions, even when there was no evidence that he had anything to do with the crime. If he declined to answer, he could be incarcerated, mutilated, or banished. In these circumstances, the decision to speak was unquestionably coerced.

Until 1878, defendants in U.S. courts were not allowed to testify at their trials because their testimony was thought to be unreliable. So, they were forced to speak in the police station and precluded from speaking in the courtroom. This was the reality that prompted enactment of the Fifth Amendment. But it was a far different reality than the one that existed in the *Griffin* case, because Griffin was free to testify.

The Court's concern was that by telling the jury it could draw reasonable inferences from Griffin's failure to testify, the trial court was in effect imposing a penalty for Griffin's silence. It undermined the Fifth Amendment privilege by making its assertion costly.

But is that in fact what happened? How does one define coercion? And is it reasonable for a jury to make no assumption when a defendant refuses to speak?

Griffin established the rule. *Carter* v. *Kentucky* took it one step further. In the early morning of December 22, 1978, Police Officer Deborah Ellison of the Hopkinsville, Kentucky, Police Department noticed movement in the alley between Young's Hardware Store and Edna's Furniture Store. She flashed her light in the alley and saw two men, who ran as she approached. She found a hole in the side of the hardware store and radioed Police Officer Leroy Davis, who spotted the two men. They ran in opposite directions and Davis apprehended one of them, Lonnie Joe Carter. Carter was charged with burglary in the third degree and with being a persistent felony offender. At the trial, Carter chose not to testify and, pursuant to *Griffin,* neither the DA nor the judge commented on his silence.

Carter's attorney, however, asked the judge that he instruct the jury with these words: "The defendant is not compelled to testify, and the fact he does not cannot be used as an inference of guilt and should not prejudice him in any way."

The judge refused the attorney's request, and Carter was found guilty and sentenced as a persistent felony offender. The Kentucky Supreme Court affirmed the conviction, holding that the requested instruction would have been tantamount to commenting on a defendant's failure to testify. But the U.S. Supreme Court disagreed, ruling that a state trial judge had a constitutional obligation, upon proper request by a defendant, to instruct the jury that it must draw no adverse inference from the defendant's failure to testify.

The law in every state today is that a judge upon request by a defendant must charge the jury that no adverse inference may be drawn from a defendant's failure to testify.

Now, there are a variety of reasons why a person might not want to testify in his own defense.

One reason may be simply that the defendant is truly innocent but is inarticulate, or unattractive, or unappealing, or he doesn't express himself well when he's nervous. I don't see that as a basis for the privilege. After all, there are lots of witnesses who might be required to testify even though they're inarticulate or unappealing. Besides, having been a trial lawyer and a trial judge for thirty-five years, my sense is that certain testimony has the ring of truth. You don't have to be educated, eloquent, or brilliant. If you're innocent and you get up and say you're innocent—and you *are* innocent—that communicates something. Often, it makes the point all the more powerfully because it is so inelegantly stated.

Another reason a person would avoid testifying is that if he testifies, his prior criminal record may be brought out. Thirty years ago, at the time *Griffin* was decided, that had greater force than it does now. In those days, a defendant's entire criminal record was brought out if he testified, even if it had nothing to do with credibility. If he spat on the sidewalk, was drunk and disorderly, whatever it was, however irrelevant to the issue of credibility, however remote in time, it would all come before the jury.

And so the defendant might say, "I'm innocent and I want to testify, but if I testify, all of this irrelevant prejudicial material will come out, and that might hurt me more than anything I might testify to."

So, over the years, that rule has been modified, and correctly so. Today, a judge is called upon in advance of a trial to advise the defendant of what in his past history is relevant and what isn't relevant. Let's say the defendant has thirty arrests and twenty-four of them are from before 1979 and we're now in 1994. Furthermore, most of the arrests were for minor offenses—disorderly conduct, drunk and disorderly, spitting on the sidewalk, marijuana possession for his own use, and so on. His current charge is robbery, so these other incidents aren't relevant.

I might rule, however, that his robbery conviction in 1992 would be relevant to his credibility in this case, and I'll allow it. But what I'll generally do when I allow use of a relevant prior conviction is to say that the attorneys may not go into the underlying facts and circumstances. Before the law was changed, it used to be that not only would the prosecution bring out the defendant's prior conviction for robbery, but they'd bring out all the underlying facts of the prior robbery, which would be extraordinarily prejudicial. He held a knife to the woman's throat. He stuck it in and she was six months pregnant at the time and her husband was in the other room. What you were really doing was retrying the other case.

So now you may bring out only the fact of a prior conviction. Most often, when the defendant does testify in his own behalf, he says, "Sure, I was convicted two or three times before and in those cases I pled guilty because I *was* guilty. But now I'm not guilty, that's why I'm going to trial today. If I were guilty I would plead guilty. But I'm not guilty. That's why I'm testifying before you now." Not a bad response, right?

So the revelation of prior convictions doesn't seem to me to be a compelling reason to avoid testifying. At the time of *Griffin,* it had more force than it has now. But we've made the system fairer, and in this regard properly so. Some commentators have gone so far as to say the defendant should be allowed to testify without any of his prior record coming in. But to me that creates the impression that he has no prior record and would wrongly bolster his credibility.

I think the compromise that we've hit on at this point in time is a decent, reasonable, and fair one. The question is, Should a judge be required to tell the jury it cannot draw inferences based on a defendant's failure to testify?

Let's return to common sense for a moment. In no other context in society do we encourage persons to withhold information. As Judge Friendly observed, "Every hour of the day people are being asked to explain their conduct to parents, employers and teachers."

The right that is being asserted is the right to withhold incriminating evidence. The irony of the argument is that we feel no such moral aversion to exploiting everyone else involved in a case except the defendant. A person may prefer not to answer questions about a murder he witnessed, but the law has never allowed such reticence. Only a person who seeks to deny the state damaging evidence about himself is protected.

We have plainly gone overboard in our efforts to protect the rights of criminal defendants. When the result is an untruth, a half truth, or a perversion of truth, we must ask if that is the right for which our forefathers struggled.

| 10 |

A JURY OF OUR FEARS

Twelve "Ordinary" Citizens the Legal System Doesn't Trust with the Truth

We have a jury system that is superior to any in the
world, and its efficacy is only marred by the difficulty
of finding twelve men every day who don't know
anything and can't read.

MARK TWAIN

The man who wants a jury has a bad case.
OLIVER WENDELL HOLMES

At a recent robbery trial, I noticed a female juror sitting with
her eyes closed during the testimony of a crucial witness. I
asked a court officer to tell her to sit with her eyes open, and
during the recess, I called her in.

"Were you sleeping?" I asked.

She shrugged.

"It's necessary for you to hear this evidence," I warned her.

"I don't really have to listen to every word," she explained,
to my dismay. "I can tell whether someone is telling the truth
by looking at the way he moves his eyebrows."

Fortunately, I learned this before the jury began to deliberate, and the juror was discharged. Yet it still troubled me. Every time I seat a jury, I fear that there is at least one person in the group who will simply not follow the rules of law. In New York, if a juror is dismissed after deliberations have started, she cannot be replaced by an alternate without the consent of the defendant—and a mistrial will almost certainly ensue. I got lucky when I caught this woman in time.

I wasn't so lucky in a case in which the defendant was charged with both murder and attempted murder. The defendant had been fired by a company that serviced automatic teller machines. While at the company, he had befriended two coworkers, with whom he drove to and from work and with whom he lunched. After being fired, he contrived to set up a false breakdown of an ATM machine in a bank in a commercial district that would be deserted after business hours. When the machine "broke," his two friends were sent out to fix it. They were unaware of the scheme, and once the ATM machine was opened (and the $80,000 in it accessible), the defendant robbed them. Though they pleaded with him, he shot each of them repeatedly and left them for dead. One of the workers survived and immediately notified the police, giving the name of the defendant as the shooter. The defendant fled the city, assumed an alias, and ultimately wound up in Canada, where he made admissions to a girlfriend, who later testified against him.

The evidence against the defendant was clear, simple, well presented, and overwhelming. Never was a man so plainly guilty.

The jury voted eleven to one for conviction, and so they remained. The holdout was convinced that the defendant was not guilty. As she explained it, "Someone that good-looking could not commit such a crime." The three-week trial was for nought, and we had to retry it. The defendant *was* convicted the second time around—within an hour.

A friend of mine recently served on a complicated conspiracy case that lasted six weeks. He reported to me that when the jury began its deliberations, one of the jurors, who had a state job that he hated, said that his mind was made up, that he would not change it, and that he would not engage in deliberations. "I don't care about going back to work," he told the other jurors. "As far as I'm concerned, we can stay here until hell freezes over." After five days, a mistrial was declared.

The jury is considered the jewel and the centerpiece of the American criminal justice system. It represents the people standing between a possibly oppressive government and the lonely, accused individual. No one can be convicted or condemned except by the judgment of his peers. By its verdict (which literally means "to speak the truth"), a community of citizens, drawn from a cross-section of the population, determines the validity of the government's charges. When we say that our system is the best in the world, we generally have the jury in mind.

But how well does the jury serve as a truth finder? How well does it serve as a voice of impartial justice? To what extent do our procedures and rules of evidence facilitate or impede the reliability of its findings?

The *rhetoric* that idealizes the jury and the *reality* of its operation are in conflict. Increasingly, we see high-profile cases of obviously guilty defendants who are acquitted by juries (the police in the Rodney King trial), or convicted of much lesser offenses (Reginald Denny). We see juries unable to reach a verdict even with the most overwhelming evidence (the Menendez brothers). Or, as in the case of O. J. Simpson, we see juries that simply fail to deliberate. And we must examine why.

Although attorneys and judges will often proclaim their admiration of a jury's ability to reach the truth, privately they will acknowledge that a trial before a jury is a crapshoot, a roll of the dice, with all the randomness and uncertainty that implies.

To some extent this is a product of the exclusionary rules and rules of evidence that we have already discussed. But to a greater extent it is a comment on the procedures by which we recruit and select jurors, and the way that we manipulate them, orient them, instruct them, and condition their behavior.

It is also a comment on the jurors themselves.

Not too long ago I heard the following "joke" twice on TV: "Remember, if you get in trouble with the law and have to go to trial, your fate will be decided by twelve people so stupid they couldn't even get out of jury duty."

Juries may be getting dumber, but it's because attorneys (especially defense attorneys) want them that way. If, as I have argued, the overwhelming number of defendants who go to trial are guilty, then it is reasonable to expect that a defense attorney will seek jurors who will not or cannot intelligently evaluate evidence. He will want gullible, manipulable, emotional, suggestible jurors—and through our system of selection he will get them.

The lie we tell ourselves about the sanctity of the jury begins with recruitment. The jury is intended to be inclusive, widely representative, and a true cross section of the community. But it is not. Most commonly, we have sought the names of prospective jurors from voter registration rolls. In a time of public apathy and cynicism, however, many citizens do not register to vote. This excludes a large percentage of the population—in many areas more than 50 percent. To deal with this problem, a number of states have sought to enlarge the rolls by obtaining the names of nonvoters from welfare rolls, tax withholding lists, and registers of licensed drivers. Some even rely on telephone directories. While the impulse to widen the base of prospective jurors is admirable, one may question whether those who will not take the brief time to vote in their own interest will be prepared to set aside a much larger block of time to sit disinterestedly on a matter that does not directly affect their lives.

Increasingly, people summoned for jury duty have not been responding. They just don't show up. For example, in the last week of July 1995, only 10 percent of those summoned to appear in the Criminal Term of the Supreme Court in New York County responded. As a result, a number of serious felony cases that were ready to proceed to trial could not go forward. What happens to those citizens who fail to respond? Nothing at all. There are no jury service enforcement officers. To my knowledge, no person has *ever* been sanctioned for a failure to respond to a jury notice. G. Thomas Munsterman, a jury expert, has stated that the only way to be caught for ignoring a jury notice is to "write in and tell the court what they can do with their summons."

Of the small number of jurors who do appear, an increasingly large number seek to be excused for reasons of convenience or necessity—especially when the trial is scheduled to last for more than a brief period. A judge will often be reluctant to refuse to excuse a prospective juror who maintains that he or she cannot serve. To refuse may only provoke the untruthful response from the juror that he cannot be fair or impartial. Long experience has taught me that to insist on a juror serving when he clearly does not want to is to assure problems in the midst of the trial.

For years, many states have had jury exemption statutes, which exempted from service certain professions or other categories of workers (doctors, lawyers, clergy). To avoid the inconvenience of jury service, some associations have sought exemptions by using political weight when there was no apparent basis for exemption. Of late, many of the states (New York most recently) have done away with these exemptions, but, for the reasons stated above, I do not expect that this expansion of the juror base will result in a larger group of available prospective jurors.

Sequestration of jurors is a relatively minor problem since it is rarely necessary and rarely utilized—the O. J. Simpson trial notwithstanding. Normally, jurors are sequestered only when it is feared they will be intimidated, endangered, or tampered with, and occasionally when a case has a very high profile.

The problem is, sequestration for long periods makes it impossible to attract and retain jurors who have families, responsible positions, good educations, and an active role in the community. Instead we get the single, the isolated, the passively employed (in bureaucratic or hierarchical jobs), and the poorly educated and ill-informed. In just those cases where the public will be most aware of whether the jury will be performing well or badly, the jury does not inspire confidence.

Once we have, with great difficulty, managed to scrape together a group of potential jurors who are willing to serve, the selection process is further complicated by the number of peremptory challenges (or challenges without cause) the lawyers are allowed. Too often, these challenges are used to "dumb down" the jury.

In 1994, I tried a case in which the defendant was charged with an $800,000 Medicaid fraud. The case was complex; it involved a great many computer printouts and bank records. The defense attorney tried to challenge three prospective jurors for cause: one was an accountant, one was the treasurer of a corporation, and the third was a math teacher. The argument was that they would be *too* knowledgeable. I denied the lawyer's challenge for cause, but he simply got rid of them with peremptory challenges. As a result of this kind of game playing, unintelligent, unsophisticated jurors are often selected to determine the "truth." The voir dire and the peremptory challenge demonstrate the basic mistrust of jurors that is held by trial lawyers.

At some level that is to be expected. The jury system requires us to entrust the fact-finding function, often in complex cases, to a group of untrained, frequently poorly educated, often reluctant and casually selected persons who are not repeat players, who do not have to give reasons or explanations for the results they reach, and who may allow extraneous considerations (the lateness of the hour, group dynamics, the appeal—or lack of it—of the lawyers) to affect their judgment.

But it is more than that. Although the Sixth Amendment requires an "impartial" jury, we have ceased in this day and age to *believe* in impartiality. And lawyers don't necessarily even want it.

In the United States, the process of jury selection is often protracted, sometimes as long as the trial itself—sometimes taking months. In the voir dire, the attorneys frequently pry into the most private areas of a juror's life. In the O. J. Simpson trial, the prospective jurors had to fill out an 80-page questionnaire with 294 questions—some calling for essay-type responses—inquiring into such compelling areas as:

- Have you ever written a letter to the editor of a newspaper or magazine?
- How important is religion in your life?
- Have you or anyone close to you undergone an amniocentesis?
- Have you ever asked a celebrity for an autograph?

Judge Lance Ito allowed the attorneys to ask whatever they wanted. These questions had nothing to do with whether a juror could be fair and impartial.

Even though it is clear that we cannot know how an individual juror will vote in any given case, we use the voir dire to indoctrinate and to pry. For lawyers whose clients have deep pockets, "scientific jury consultants" are increasingly relied upon. It is now a growing industry—with polls and focus groups and shadow juries. And, increasingly, we are eliminating jurors on the basis of group biases.

I don't support the elimination of peremptory challenges altogether, for the simple reason that we need a way to dismiss a person who may be technically acceptable but whose tone, posture, or manner is just not right. Yet I feel strongly that we should limit these challenges to three for each side.

The experience with the peremptory challenge in England may be instructive. The prosecution has not had any peremptory challenges since 1305. Apparently, Parliament felt that the peremptory challenge allowed the government to obtain juries that favored the government. But it did continue to allow the defendant peremptory challenges.

Nevertheless, over the centuries, Parliament reduced the number of peremptory challenges available to the defense. Originally, the defendant was provided thirty-five peremptory challenges, but by 1530 that was reduced to twenty (except for treason). This was later reduced to seven and then, in 1977, to three. Finally, in 1988, Parliament abolished the defendant's peremptory challenge altogether. Judge Raymond Broderick has written: "Concern that defense lawyers were manipulating the peremptory challenge to pack juries with biased individuals, thereby defeating the ability of random draw techniques to ensure a representative petit jury, supplied the impetus behind the revision."

In our own country, the peremptory challenge has historically been used to ensure that African Americans and members of other minority groups did not appear on the jury. In the 1932 Scottsboro case, discussed earlier, where nine black men were accused of raping two white women, records showed that in the prior fifty years no black had ever served on a jury in the two relevant Alabama counties.

In fact, it should be clear that the expansive use of the peremptory challenge is inherently incompatible with the random and fair cross-section principle of jury selection.

The irony is that as we have enlarged eligibility for jury service as a manifestation of our faith in the democratic and popular administration of justice, the peremptory challenge reflects our ambivalence, doubt, and mistrust.

In 1986, in *Batson* v. *Kentucky,* the U.S. Supreme Court recognized that the unlimited peremptory challenge had become a vehicle for discrimination. Through *Batson* and its progeny, the Court has sought to limit the exercise of peremptory challenges by both prosecution and defense attorneys on both racial and gender grounds, but it did not do this by abolishing the peremptory challenge. Instead, it permitted inquiry into the *motives* of the attorneys when they exercise a peremptory challenge—and thus created, both procedurally and substantively, what one court observer has called an "enforcement nightmare." Trial judges are left at sea without guidance to determine—or guess—whether the peremptory challenges exercised by the parties were based on race or gender, or whether they were racially or gender "neutral." The procedures we must engage in to make these findings prolong the trial and leave each trial's finality uncertain—hostage to whether an appellate court will later find that the trial court guessed correctly.

It is an intolerable situation. At a judicial conference I recently attended, hours were occupied trying to figure out the procedural and substantive implications of *Batson*. Most frightening was the number of times the instructors responded to intelligent questions from trial judges with, "I don't know—we'll have to wait and find out." As we try to make it more fair, the system becomes more time-consuming, more complex, more unknowable, and more uncertain. Truth becomes less central. The issue of the defendant's guilt becomes more and more subordinate. "Did he do it" becomes lost in the mélange of other issues—and the other issues come to dominate not only the trial but the appeal.

Reducing the number of peremptory challenges to three severely limits the role of discriminatory jury selection, curtails the time we will spend on voir dire, and yet provides some flexibility to remove those jurors for whom a challenge for cause is not warranted but about whom there is some basis for feeling unease. It would also largely do away with the problems created by *Batson*. And it would undercut the rationale for "scientific" jury consultants—something I, for one, would like to see.

Erratic and irrational jury behavior make verdicts a crapshoot. But a jury trial is also a minefield where the search for truth can be waylaid and blown up by a multitude of rules that are arbitrary and serve no useful purpose—least of all to aid us in the search for the truth.

Evidence is admissible in a trial only if it is relevant. A judge determines relevance by asking whether the proffered evidence assists in establishing a fact in issue or in controverting it. But not all relevant evidence is admissible. Sometimes relevant evidence is highly prejudicial but only minimally probative.

If we had complete faith in the ability of the jury to function as mature, sophisticated, and intelligent fact finders, then we could submit to them *all* relevant evidence, but we don't have that faith.

So the judge serves as a gatekeeper. He decides not only what is relevant but also whether the jury will be able to hear *all* of the relevant evidence.

In 1994 I had a case where the defendant was accused of strangling a woman to death with a copper wire (murder). He then set her body on fire in her apartment (arson), then shot a female witness in the eye (attempted murder).

The sole witness was the wounded woman—a crack addict with a severe head injury and only one eye. She was, by all accounts, a poor witness, so the prosecution was looking for additional ways to make its case.

There were four crime-scene photos that showed the burned-out apartment and the remains of the victim—charred beyond recognition. Even her human form had lost definition.

Prior to jury selection, the defense attorney sought a ruling that would preclude the district attorney from showing the photos to a jury on the grounds that their prejudicial impact would exceed their probative value. He argued that the pictures were "inflammatory," which they certainly were, in more ways than one. He argued that the only issue in the case was the identification of the defendant as the perpetrator, so the photos had no evidential value.

The district attorney responded that the credibility of the witness—the one-eyed crack addict—was the heart of her case. The photos would corroborate her version of how the events took place—where the fire was set, where the copper wire was placed—and thereby bolster the witness's identification of the defendant as the perpetrator.

I handled this request by permitting the use of one photo—the one that was the least gruesome yet depicted the areas of the DA's concern, and I excluded the other three photos.

The DA also wanted to introduce a passport-type photo of the victim so that she would have a human face for the jury. I allowed this request as it seemed harmless enough. Although the photo would have no great relevance, neither would it be prejudicial. I am not opposed to letting a jury know who the victim is. The New York Court of Appeals, however, has said that this would be error, out of concern that the jury wouldn't be able to properly assess it. We are forever shielding the tender eyes of the jury from the harsh realities of the truth.

Because we do not trust the jury to sift that which is probative from that which is prejudicial, we exclude relevant evidence from the jury when the judge concludes that the prejudicial impact of the evidence exceeds its probative value.

Sometimes even when the evidence is *highly* probative, it is excluded because it is "too inflammatory." The case of *Johnson* v. *United States* is a good example.

The evidence showed that Johnson, after murdering one individual, went to the victim's apartment and shot the victim's thirteen-year-old son along with another child. The Federal District of Columbia Court of Appeals found this evidence more prejudicial than probative of Johnson being the first victim's killer and reversed his murder conviction.

Note, however, that the murder of the children tended in several ways to establish that Johnson was guilty of the first killing:

1. The same weapon was used to murder all three individuals.
2. Johnson was familiar with the apartment and its occupants.
3. A weapon taken from the victim's apartment was in Johnson's possession at the time of his arrest.

Nevertheless, the majority held that the trial court had erred in admitting the evidence. "The emotional impact of the heinous slaying of two innocent children, asleep and alone in an apartment" was simply too inflammatory. It was determined that the prejudicial impact of this evidence outweighed its probative value. It was, in my opinion, a maddening decision.

Contrast *Johnson* with the issue of the admissibility of the Fuhrman tapes in the O. J. Simpson case. You'll recall that Judge Ito allowed the playing of tapes from a past interview in which Fuhrman used racial slurs. The tendency in this area of the law to be more generous to the defendant than to the People is manifest. The People can't appeal an acquittal, but the defendant can appeal a conviction. Precisely because of this fact, the People ought to be given the benefit of the doubt on issues of law, and the defendant the benefit of the doubt on issues of fact.

The Fuhrman tapes were certainly more prejudicial than probative. They were not fundamental to the main proof of the case and would unduly prejudice a mostly African-American jury. Yet Judge Ito deemed them relevant.

The necessity of unanimity from twelve jurors has continued to be a source of frustration in the court's ability to carry out justice.

A few years ago in the Bronx Supreme Court, Ray Donovan, a former secretary of labor in the Reagan administration, was accused with others of an elaborate conspiracy. By all accounts the case was not a strong one, but it was a long one, lasting about six months.

As you know, trial judges almost always empanel alternate jurors, so that a trial will not have to be aborted if a regularly selected juror is discharged or must be excused, and this had been done in *Donovan.*

In *Donovan,* after the six-month trial, the judge charged the jury and they retired to deliberate. Within fifteen minutes one of the female jurors had a nervous breakdown. She was found banging her head against the wall in the ladies' room, and had to be removed in a straitjacket.

Under New York law, a jury of eleven cannot render a verdict. Also under New York law, alternates cannot be present in the jury room when regular jurors deliberate. And once a jury has begun to deliberate, no alternate juror is permitted to substitute for a regular juror who has been discharged without the defendant's written consent.

The judge in *Donovan* called all the parties before him and proposed that an alternate juror substitute for the discharged regular juror. The defendants opposed this suggestion and refused to consent. Under the law, the judge had no legal alternative but to declare a mistrial—an unhappy and wasteful outcome to be sure.

Instead, the judge conferred with his administrative superior and decided in spite of the law to substitute an alternate. This was risky, but the judge thought the case was weak and the jury would probably acquit. If it convicted Donovan, the judge could always set the verdict aside because of his (deliberate) error of law—and he would be no worse off than if he did not substitute the alternate.

The jury acquitted Donovan and the others shortly after the alternate was seated.

This was indeed an inspired, practical, and unlawful response to an absurd law. Yet in spite of the attention the case received at the time, our legislature has made no effort to change the law.

A similar situation arose in my courtroom. In my case, the evidence against the accused was overwhelming. The trial was relatively brief. The major witness, who had relocated, had to be flown in from out-of-state at some expense to the state and inconvenience to the witness. Shortly after deliberations began, after the jury had disbanded for the night, a juror in her seventh month of pregnancy developed complications that precluded her continued service. The alternates had been discharged because the defendant had said he would under no circumstances consent to any replacement. Although both sides consented to eleven jurors rendering a verdict, the law precluded that, and I was required to declare a mistrial. Parenthetically, while these matters were being discussed in the court, the jurors had continued their deliberation. Prior to the break the night before, the jurors had voted eleven to one for conviction, and the lone dissenter had changed her mind. So at the time they were discharged, they stood unanimously for conviction.

Although the U.S. Constitution does not require unanimous verdicts, and although thirty-three states permit non-unanimous verdicts in civil cases, forty-eight of our fifty states require unanimous verdicts in criminal cases, and so do the federal courts.

It's hard to know why this is so; it is simply a subject we don't discuss. It's a sacred cow. Two years ago the chief judge of the state of New York empaneled a commission to study the working of the jury system and to recommend changes. After much study the commission issued a lengthy report. When I looked at the report to see what it had to say about unanimity, it said that the subject had not been taken up because it was "controversial." One might argue that that is exactly why it *should* have been taken up! But the committee clearly wanted to avoid opening that particular can of worms.

Why can't we discuss the legitimacy of unanimous juries? What would happen if we allowed verdicts of ten to two or eleven to one? This is certainly far more than a bare majority. Would the search for truth be impaired? Would the jury system lose legitimacy and respect—more than it already has? Would the deliberative process be affected adversely?

Presumably, there would be fewer hung juries—so the system would be more efficient. Would it be less fair? Because jury deliberations are secret, exhaustive studies are not possible. The most highly regarded study was done by Harry Kalven, Jr., and Hans Zeisel in their work *The American Jury,* published in 1966. Kalven and Zeisel concluded that deliberation had no significant effect on the final verdict in nine out of ten cases. "With very few exceptions the first ballot determines the outcome of the verdict . . . the real decision is often made before the deliberation begins." The authors also concluded that deliberation did not change votes through reasoning, but rather through intimidation and peer pressure. In that sense, unanimity should not lead us to conclude that the verdict is more reliable.

A study by Dr. Deanna Kuhn of Columbia University Teachers College in New York, published in 1994 in the journal *Psychological Science,* showed that substantial numbers of jurors often jumped to conclusions early in the case and then tended to stick vehemently with those conclusions. These decision makers were largely immune to the deliberative process.

Justice Lewis Powell concluded that the unanimity rule put pressure on jurors to compromise, "despite the frequent absence of a rational basis for such compromise." So that in the end the requirement of unanimity led "not to full agree-ment among the twelve but to agreement by none and com-promise by all." Greater accuracy might be obtained without a dissenter's veto, and without the need to compromise with one or two holdouts who resist reasoned argument.

My own experience as a trial judge leads me to agree with this assessment. In every instance that I can recall where the jury was split ten to two or eleven to one, in my judgment the holdout was *not* being rational. On the other hand, when the split was eight to four or seven to five, both sides had a reasoned basis for their positions.

In the interest of truth and efficiency, I would recommend permitting verdicts of eleven to one or ten to two.

This problem with alternates, unanimity, and the magic number twelve pervades our system and often impedes the search for truth. So does the minefield of technicalities. An example of this occurred in my courtroom some years ago.

The defendant was accused of forgery. He possessed a stolen credit card, which had the photo of the cardholder affixed to it. The defendant substituted his own photo for that of the rightful owner, and proceeded to an appliance store where he attempted to purchase a large number of items with the card. When the clerk sought approval for the transaction, he learned that the card had been reported stolen. The defendant was detained by store security.

The case was very strong against the defendant. He was caught in the act, he had put his own picture on the stolen card, and the owner of the card testified that he had not given permission or authority for the defendant to use the card. The defendant offered no evidence and no defense.

In my instructions to the jury, I had to explain a number of matters of law, including the five essential elements of forgery, which the People were required to prove beyond a reasonable doubt.

Within five minutes of retiring to deliberate, the jury requested a rereading of the five elements of forgery, and three or four of the jurors wished to write them down.

Neither side objected and I repeated the elements—speaking slowly and carefully so that the jurors could write accurately what I said.

Within the hour the jury returned a verdict of guilty. This verdict was reversed on appeal, because the appellate court felt that the jurors who wrote down the elements would have disproportionate and unwarranted influence over those who did not take notes!

Increasingly, our New York Court of Appeals has taken, as Paul Shectman, New York State Director of Criminal Justice, has said, "the view that a criminal defendant is entitled not only to a fair trial, but to a perfect one" and that *any* imperfection requires a retrial regardless of whether the defendant has been prejudiced by the error. The result is a proliferation of per se rules (rules that require reversal without reference to whether the defendant has been harmed).

The *Spivey* case, decided in July 1993, is a fine example of this trend.

Dwayne Spivey was arrested for a robbery that occurred on a crowded midtown Manhattan street. A police officer observed the crime in progress and arrested Spivey before he could flee. Two accomplices fled to a subway station, where they were arrested after a struggle in which a police officer was injured.

Spivey was charged with two counts of robbery in the second degree. One count was that Spivey was "aided by another" and the second count was that he had "caused physical injury" to a nonparticipant in the crime.

After the judge instructed the jury he provided them with a verdict sheet that listed the charges. To make it clear what the different counts meant, he added in parentheses after Count One "another person present," and after Count Two "caused physical injury to nonparticipant." The judge told the jury that these parentheticals were designed to help them distinguish between the different counts. When the defense attorney objected, the judge explained that the jurors would have no other way of telling the difference.

Shortly thereafter, the jury convicted Spivey of attempted robbery in the second degree. The conviction was reversed on the ground that an "annotated" verdict sheet had been submitted. The New York Court of Appeals held that "unless the parties agree, it is reversible (not harmless) error to give the jury a verdict sheet listing some of the statutory elements of the counts."

Blessedly, no other state in the country—and no federal court—has found this to be reversible error. Annotated verdict sheets are generally thought to promote justice. They aid juries in differentiating the charges. But allowing an annotated verdict sheet is now per se reversible error in New York.

The failure to make annotated verdict sheets "harmless error" has meant scores of retrials. As of August 1993, thirty-four convictions had been overturned, including several *murder* convictions in which the verdict sheet bore the simple annotation "felony murder" and "intentional murder" in parentheses next to the two otherwise identical counts. It's insane.

We have assigned awesome responsibility and power to this group of twelve "ordinary" citizens, whom we do not trust with the truth—and indeed strive to mislead. More and more, other factors outside the law are seeping into jury boxes and making the outcome of criminal trials more questionable as jurors assert their power without restraint.

Under our law, jurors are told by the judge that they are *only* finders of fact and that they are obliged by their oath to accept the law as the judge gives it to them, to apply that law to the facts they have found, and thereby reach their verdict.

In fact, jurors have the power to ignore a judge's instructions and to do whatever they please. Judges don't tell them this, and they don't permit the attorneys to tell them either. But jury deliberations are secret, and jurors can never be punished for the way they vote (or don't vote)—and many jurors know of this power. Of late, an organization called the Fully Informed Jury Association (FIJA) has begun to lobby for laws protecting the "right" of nullification—and, more importantly, to advise citizens and prospective jurors of that power. Many who are involved in violating one law or another are expected to respond favorably to such an initiative.

The problem is especially urgent and a matter of concern now when we appear to be witnessing racial line-drawing during jury deliberations. Although jury nullification has been employed to restrain a tyrannical government, it is a double-edged sword, one that has been used to exonerate Southern whites who killed or injured blacks and civil rights workers and also to condemn blacks in the South and elsewhere on insufficient evidence. When the government is democratic and not oppressive, nullification mocks the rule of law.

Although, when we speak of nullification, we generally have in mind the action of the *entire* jury, we should also understand that isolated jurors can also act to nullify without regard to the law or the evidence. The unanimity requirement enhances their power and enlarges their role.

Whatever the demographic makeup of a community may be, the law does not require that the final jury of twelve reflect the exact proportion of each group in the population. (In polyglot New York City, we would probably need a jury of fifty to serve that end.) The law has aimed to be inclusive, and no group can reasonably claim that it is being excluded.

But, increasingly, our search for a jury that is truly representative of the community has involved us in issues of race, gender, national origin, and religion. The theory behind the jury was that through a cross section of the population we obtain diverse and enriching perspectives—and that the jurors, once selected, would impartially, disinterestedly, and objectively seek the truth.

The large number of peremptory challenges has always imperiled that goal and has allowed its discriminatory impact to skew the composition of the final group of twelve. Only the abolition of the peremptory challenge, or its substantial reduction, can deal with the consequences of its abuse.

But we are also at another crossroads. We must examine whether the jury will be a deliberative body or a representative one; whether its members will see themselves as part of a group, proportionately represented and designated to vote a certain way, or whether they will see themselves as impartial, disinterested, and focused entirely on the evidence.

The divisions in a multiethnic society cannot be resolved by the criminal justice system—just as conditions outside of the criminal justice system provide us with the defendants who inhabit it. If the racial, cultural, and class divisions continue to multiply and intensify, there can be no doubt that they will impact on the jury to its lasting detriment.

Ours is the only system in the world that gives such absolute power to a jury of ordinary citizens.

Japan, for example, had a jury system for a while and dropped it. Israel has never had one. Germany, France, and most of the rest of Europe rely on small panels of professional and lay judges. India inherited the British jury system from its former colonizers, but dropped it in 1961.

Shortly before Mikhail Gorbachev left office, at the invitation of the Lawyers Committee for Human Rights, I and two federal judges went to the then U.S.S.R. We found an enormous interest in our jury system from the judges, lawyers, and academics that we met. Although Russia had a jury system under the tsars, it had been abandoned under the Bolsheviks in favor of a mixed panel of professional and lay judges. The professionals with whom we met admired the jury system and considered it a protection against the tyranny from which they were just then emerging. I understand that Russia is now experimenting with a jury system.

England has a jury system. But it seems to be plagued by some of the same problems we face in America. Consider how a London jury resolved the issues in a recent murder case.

After being unable to reach a decision on the first day of deliberation, the jury was sent to a hotel. While there, four jurors convened and used a Ouija board to make contact with the murder victim. (Since they didn't have a Ouija board in the room, they fashioned one by printing letters of the alphabet on scraps of paper and using a glass instead of a pointer.) The jurors each put a finger on the glass, which then purportedly moved toward a succession of letters, revealing, it was claimed, a message from the deceased: "Vote guilty tomorrow."

At breakfast the following morning the matter was discussed with other members of the jury. The result was a unanimous verdict to convict. The conviction was later reversed on appeal and the defendant was retried and convicted again—this time in the conventional manner. Judging from what I see every day in the courtroom, jurors might just as well use Ouija boards to reach their decisions.

JUDGMENT DAY

A Demand for Common Sense
in the Courtroom

Justice is truth in action.
BENJAMIN DISRAELI

During the period I was writing this book, the O. J. Simpson trial was running in the background. It was ironic, to say the least. Although commentators often assured the public that this trial was an aberration whose bizarreness, pettiness, length, and disorganization were not common to "normal" courtrooms, I saw it another way. As the weeks and months progressed, the Simpson trial became for me a sterling example of everything that is wrong with our criminal justice system rolled into one spectacular event. We can't let ourselves off the hook by saying it was unusual—for it is precisely the same formalism and complexity of our criminal law that plague all trials that allowed in this one the most egregious behavior.

On the face of it, this was a murder case not unlike many that have come through my courtroom. Murder is ugly but not uncommon. During my years on the bench, I have seen a gruesome parade of bodies—riddled with bullet holes, smashed into unrecognizable pulp, torn apart with knives. And too often I have witnessed the fatal outcome of once loving relationships gone terribly wrong. The trial of O. J. Simpson was certainly not "the trial of the century" in the sense that it represented an unusual crime. The only difference here was that the defendant was a celebrity with seemingly bottomless resources, and a defendant certainly has a right to purchase the best defense he can afford. However, in this case, I think the public realized something was dreadfully wrong. As the months wore on and the public obsession grew, it was quite apparent that the trial of O. J. Simpson was unveiling the scandal of our courtrooms. The level of absurdity reached in the Simpson trial may not go on in every courtroom, but the point is, it *can*.

On October 3, 1995, after nine months of sequestration and less than four hours of deliberation, the jury voted unanimously to acquit O. J. Simpson of the double murder of his ex-wife Nicole Brown and her friend Ronald Goldman. In the aftermath of this disgraceful show, the nation was left feeling wounded and deeply distrustful of the system. On the day of the verdict, time stopped for a moment while we all listened for the result. Around the criminal courthouse on

Centre Street in New York there was a solemn mood that day, a feeling of betrayal among the hardworking men and women whose task is justice.

The verdict itself was not the reason for dismay. We have all seen defendants acquitted when we believed they were guilty. Our system demands that we hold prosecutors to the highest standards of proof, and we wouldn't want it any other way. But there was something dreadfully wrong with the process that led to this verdict. We like to say that our system is the best in the world. But few people viewed the O. J. Simpson trial as an example of the best. In almost every way, it highlighted the worst in our system and in ourselves.

From the start, Simpson's trial looked and sounded more like theater than law. The preliminary hearings lasted nearly five months and jury selection took six weeks. If every murder trial in America took this long, our justice system would literally grind to a halt. It certainly makes a joke of the speedy trial statutes and puts more pressure on an already burdened system. In fact, California has a speedy trial statute that allowed Simpson to demand a trial within ninety days. He did so, I believe, because he thought the DA couldn't effectively prepare its case within that time, and the early trial would throw them off. This is a clear example of how speedy trial statutes are used in a manipulative way. A judge should have the discretion to afford each party a reasonable time to prepare. Ninety days might be enough time in some cases, but not in all. These arbitrary time periods are a straitjacket, an affront to a well-reasoned and thoughtful process.

During the lengthy preliminary hearings, prosecutors and detectives involved in the investigation had their feet put to the fire over the manner in which the search was conducted—the main question being: Should detectives have gone over the wall at Simpson's estate without first obtaining a search warrant? We've already discussed in this book how complex and unknowable the search-and-seizure laws have become. Critics of the police action in the Simpson case are asking for superhuman wisdom from the very human police officers who had just viewed a horribly bloody crime scene. Do we really think they should have paused at length to ponder Fourth Amendment questions in which the judiciary itself is in disagreement? Those police were damned if they did go over the wall, and equally damned if they didn't. There is no right answer. I believe the police acted according to their best professional judgment. They did not have the luxury of lengthy perusal of thousands of pages of Fourth Amendment arguments brought to the court. Judge Lance Ito was correct to allow the evidence obtained at Simpson's Rockingham estate, but in retrospect, it probably didn't matter. The defense managed to successfully paint a picture of ill-intentioned police action anyway. The leap over Simpson's wall became, in the defense team's rhetoric, a dark and suspicious action—perhaps even part of a police conspiracy. And the jury bought it.

Moreover, if there was any hope at all that the trial of O. J. Simpson would be a search for the truth, it was dashed the moment defense attorney Johnnie Cochran introduced the issue of race. In my opinion, the argument that a racist policeman (or policemen) deliberately framed an African

American in the city of Los Angeles, without having any real evidence to support it, was a contemptuous strategy. While it is true that defense attorneys have a primary loyalty to their clients, they can't simply ignore ethics and decency in the process. Good lawyers should not be bad citizens. It was their responsibility, if they believed racism was a legitimate defense, to offer evidence of that fact. Instead, they used innuendo and suggestion to fan the flames of an already tense racial environment, creating, they hoped, enough smoke to mask the question: Did O. J. Simpson commit these murders?

It is a judge's role to make sure that information presented to the jury is real evidence, is more probative than prejudicial, and that it has a basis in fact. This did not happen at the Simpson trial. Had it been my courtroom, I would have demanded that the defense attorneys offer some foundation beyond mere speculation for their belief that Detective Mark Fuhrman planted a bloody glove at Simpson's house, and that other police officers were involved in a conspiracy to convict Simpson. It is not enough to say, "It *might* have happened." Nor is it enough to say, "It *could* have happened." It is not even enough to say, "Fuhrman would have liked to do it." If speculation were allowed to become evidence in a trial, juries would become hopelessly confused.

Likewise, the suggestion that Simpson's arrest and prosecution was a "rush to judgment" was absurd. The probability screens were well in place before Simpson was brought to trial. I have rarely seen in my own courtroom facts so strong and compelling regarding motive, opportunity, and abundant circumstantial evidence.

Throughout the trial, the behavior of the lawyers on both sides was distracting and unprofessional, in the courtroom and outside. From the defense position, it was a daily game of focusing attention on everything but O. J. Simpson's guilt or innocence.

The use of media was a cynical strategy. Perhaps it was a way of leaking information to the jurors, who might be tainted during conjugal visits. Or at the very least, it was an effort to taint the next jury pool should a hung jury necessitate a second trial.

Judges get the lawyers they deserve. If they tolerate misconduct they have it in abundance. If they don't run their courtrooms, then the lawyers will—with all the chaos that implies. I can still recall my dismay, early in the Simpson trial, when I heard Judge Ito tell defense attorney Peter Neufeld, "That's the *thirteenth* time I've asked you not to ask that question." I thought he sounded like an impotent parent who is full of threats but never carries them out. When Neufeld later appeared in my own courtroom, I warned him, "Peter, you're not even going to get past the *first* time." He shrugged and said, "Don't blame me. Judge Ito let me do it."

The judge's duty is to strive for the correct result, properly arrived at. He has an interest in seeing that the process operates rationally, and that jurors are not tricked or misled. Committed to the search for truth, the judge is also required by the rules of the game to sit by helplessly while skilled professionals are engaged in clear, deliberate, and entirely "proper" efforts to frustrate the search.

Our criminal process embraces as a chief value the protection of the innocent, and we have built an elaborate set of barriers that the prosecution must surmount before it can arrive at a conviction that will stand up on appeal. It is an obstacle course, a struggle from start to finish.

The trial judge, though ostensibly charged with the leadership of a proceeding that is to conclude in a "speaking of the truth" (i.e., a *verdict*), is, at the same time, mandated by rules to often sit by helplessly while attorneys are visibly engaged in an attempt to twist or foreclose the truth—and this is a matter of shared understanding between court and counsel, concealed only from the jury.

Let's look at the Simpson jury itself. The high-profile nature of the trial, coupled with the lengthy sequestration, made it impossible to construct a jury of average citizens. Right away, there was a bias toward people who were uneducated, disengaged from community life, and perhaps even eager to be a part of such a big case. In the course of the trial, several jurors were excused for making efforts to sell book contracts—and two of them wrote books even before the trial was over.

In the aftermath of the trial, jurors rushed to sign up with agents for book and movie deals. They appeared on prime-time television interviews, and one dismissed juror agreed to pose nude for *Playboy*. What does this say about our system when twelve citizens, charged with a task of utmost seriousness, become celebrities themselves and are allowed to posture in front of the cameras like grand-lottery winners? Although the First Amendment allows every citizen the right to speak publicly, write books, and appear in movies, there is something unseemly about what has occurred with these jurors. If we are to respect the jury system as an honest and untainted means to a verdict, we cannot ignore the possibility that ordinary people might be swayed by extraordinary opportunity.

Furthermore, if you doubt that Simpson's defense lawyers successfully used their peremptory challenges to construct a jury of the most uneducated and easily swayed, you need only listen to the posttrial interviews with the jurors. What struck me immediately, as I listened to the jurors explain their verdict, was that they were remarkably poor evaluators of the facts. There was little commonsense evaluation of the questions raised about the evidence. In their comments, they discounted the mountain of DNA evidence as though it were of no significance, and based their poorly understood definition of reasonable doubt on a careless and brief perusal of what was said at trial. They made no distinction between factual evidence and attorney suggestion. And they surely did not subject defense arguments to a rigorous review.

For example, most of the jurors agreed that they had reasonable doubt based on the possibility that the glove and other evidence were planted. But none of them followed a logical thought process to determine if that were really a possibility. To reach a valid conclusion of reasonable doubt, they would have had to conduct a lengthy analysis of the conduct of all the investigators and laboratory technicians. Indeed, there were so many separate pieces of evidence that it seems virtually impossible that they could all have been planted— even if there was a motive to do so.

It also appears that at least some of the jurors ignored Judge Ito's instruction that domestic violence could be considered as a motive. "What does domestic violence have to do with murder?" asked one juror. Her attitude was appalling to many, but it was also an example of the power juries have to simply ignore or nullify the law when they deliberate.

The jurors who have spoken publicly defend their verdict passionately. But say what they might, it is clear to me that this jury failed in its single assigned task: to deliberate on the evidence and reach an informed decision. This was jury nullification, plain and simple. They chose not to deliberate. In our system of justice, we allow juries this kind of power, and it troubles many of us who are concerned about fairness and truth. It's no surprise that after the verdict Johnnie Cochran singled out the paid jury consultant as the hero of the case.

O. J. Simpson's silence in the courtroom, contrasted with his outspokenness after the trial, was also disturbing to many. For nine months, Simpson sat in the courtroom, in full view of the jury, and listened to the testimony of many witnesses. In the end, he remained silent, and that was his constitutional right. Furthermore, Judge Ito was charged by law to instruct the jury that it may draw no inferences from his silence. But Simpson's silence left many unanswered questions that a jury, sequestered for nine months, might have reasonably wanted answered.

What would be so wrong with a system that requested a defendant to testify in a court of law, on the record, and in the presence of his lawyers and the judge, after a showing of his probable guilt had been demonstrated by the evidence? Why were we not entitled to hear O. J. Simpson under these circumstances? Criminalist Dennis Fung was on the witness stand for nine days, and Simpson not at all. Surely Simpson had relevant information to provide a jury that was seeking the truth. Surely the testimony in a courtroom is less subject to abuse than the incommunicado questioning of a suspect in the police station. And if Simpson did not speak, why should the jury not have been instructed by Judge Ito that they might draw an adverse inference from his failure to deny or explain the evidence against him?

It offends our sense of common decency that as soon as the trial was over, Simpson was eager to communicate. In the public forum, he couldn't wait to speak. His most bizarre statement came when he told *The New York Times* that he was challenging prosecutor Marcia Clark to a pay-per-view debate. "I'd like to be able to knock that chip off Marcia's shoulder," he said gleefully, as if the real nature of the process was a sporting contest.

Clark replied coolly to Simpson's challenge by saying, "I already invited him to talk to me during the trial, and he declined."

What have we learned from the O. J. Simpson trial about the pursuit of justice in our society?

- That power and money have the effect of creating elaborate screens that hide the truth.
- That jury selection is hostage to peremptory challenges that, with the help of scientific jury experts, can mold a

jury in the hope that it will be swayed by emotion and innuendo, not fact.

- That trial by media is a real specter in the age of unrestrained tabloid journalism.
- That clever defense attorneys, coupled with passive judges, can fashion "evidence" out of innuendo.
- That the only person who is protected from having to explain himself and his actions is the very person who is accused of the crime—and who may know the most about it.
- That juries are fragile bodies, subject to emotion, suggestion, and speculation, and that often juries are comprised of citizens who lack the capacity to intelligently evaluate evidence.
- That the American courtroom is dangerously out of order.

A criminal trial is society's way of seeking justice when the life and liberty of its citizens are jeopardized. Can we be satisfied that this happened in the Simpson trial? The answer is a resounding no!

I am not afraid to say what is unquestionably true: that justice was not done in this case. O. J. Simpson is free. He will never be criminally prosecuted for these murders again. And society is left with the bitter taste of perverse justice. By law, Simpson is not guilty. Our system, however, *is* guilty, and it is the people who are punished.

This is my thirty-seventh year in criminal law—twelve years as a defense attorney and twenty-five years as a trial judge presiding over criminal cases. For as long as I can remember, practicing criminal law and being involved with this process is what I wanted to do. Nothing, it seemed to me, could be more exciting and stimulating, intellectually and personally, than being present at a meeting between the state and its citizens at moments of extreme conflict. And nothing could be more important.

But I am often discouraged. Over the last thirty-five years, since the advent of the Warren Court (which reacted to abuses that existed at that time), we have witnessed changes in constitutional interpretation and procedural statutes that have substantially altered the balance of advantage in criminal cases to favor the accused. As a result, we have made unduly elaborate and effective the means of blocking the proof of guilt.

The stories in this book have illustrated how complex, arbitrary, irrational, and incomprehensible our law can be—how, increasingly, it resembles a lottery. We now exclude highly reliable and probative evidence routinely and we impose unnecessary, unreasonable, and arbitrary limits on the power of the police. We authorize our lawyers to engage in truth-defeating trickery and distortion.

This book is replete with cases where an obviously guilty, and often violent, criminal goes free. These results, and the shoddy reasoning that is frequently relied on to support them, should be intolerable in a civilized (and menaced) society with a highly developed system of law.

In spite of what must be an increasing awareness of these defects and deficits, we somehow, against all the evidence, continue to repeat the mantra that ours is the "best" system

in the world. Whether we say this out of arrogance, igno-
rance, or inertia is unclear.

To the citizenry, the system is largely unknowable and
inaccessible—and we have been taught from earliest childhood to view it with reverence and without question. My
law school students are quick to mock the Ten Command-
ments—or at least some of them—but the first ten Amendments to the Constitution, the Bill of Rights, is holy writ and
not to be questioned or critically examined.

Those working within the system are self-interested or have
institutional interests they are determined to defend. They are
often quick to question the motives, values, or competence of
those who would challenge things as they are. Some principles, procedures, and practices are held to be sacrosanct.

This book is a call to look at our system afresh: to see it
clearly; to review its workings; to rethink its present principles, prescriptions, and practices; and to ask *whether* we
have the "best" system—or whether we deserve better.

Although we are a democracy, we have deferred these
questions to our high priests (the judges), who tell us the
meaning of our bible (the Constitution). Perhaps because it
seems so difficult to change it, we are disinclined to question
it. And when dissident voices are raised, there is a concerted
cacophony that is quick to question their motives and values.

Because of the power of precedent, even the U.S. Supreme
Court is reluctant to overrule holdings where it has doubts as
to whether its decisions serve their intended purposes. That's
how the exclusionary rule and the *Miranda* rule, among
others, become fixed and immovable icons in our temple of
justice. It appears that we are locked in place.

England, in the light of its experience, has done away with the peremptory challenge and the unanimous verdict and now permits a jury to draw an adverse inference from a defendant's silence, but we have not even begun to seriously contemplate such changes. There is a scarcity of comparative studies of the criminal justice systems of the British Commonwealth, Scandinavia, and the countries of Western Europe. The fine scholars who work in this area are largely ignored by the legal profession and legislators. We are possessed by a feeling of superiority in relation to these systems. As Professor Rudolf Schlesinger has written, this feeling "seems to grow in direct proportion to the ever-increasing weight of the accumulating evidence demonstrating the total failure of our system of criminal justice."

The public dissatisfaction with the administration of criminal justice today is well founded. It reflects a proper perception that our courts have substituted formalism for fairness, and, in the process, they are burying the truth. There is also, I believe, a growing, though as yet unexpressed, dissatisfaction on the part of our trial judges.

Not long ago I attended a judicial conference where one of the subjects on which we were lectured concerned a notice statute. The statute required the prosecutor to provide notice to the defendant, within fifteen days of his arraignment, of any statements the prosecutor intended to introduce at trial and of any prior identifications that he would be relying upon. The highest appellate court in New York had construed the statute to *preclude* the prosecutor from using this evidence if the notice was filed after the fifteenth day or, even if filed in a timely fashion, if it was incomplete in the details it provided. Even if the defendant had not been harmed or prejudiced in any way, the appellate court held that the evidence—the truth—had to be kept from the jury. As a result of these rulings, many violent felons have been released.

This was more than just an obscure, theoretical debate. We discussed a specific case that had occurred in New York the previous year. José Lopez had entered a woman's apartment intending to burglarize it, but when he unexpectedly found her at home he stabbed her in the chest with a large kitchen knife. Lopez was later identified by the woman, he confessed his guilt, and a jury convicted him of the crime. But his conviction was overturned by the New York Court of Appeals because the DA's pretrial notice of evidence was deemed to contain insufficient detail.

For two hours we listened to three erudite instructors talk about when such notice is required and what the notice must contain. At the end of their talk, I rose to thank our teachers for their presentation, and went on to bemoan the fact that as we approach the end of the twentieth century, American jurists had to be preoccupied by such arcana. I said it was obscene that we were releasing those charged with serious crimes, without regard to the evidence of their guilt, because a notice was a day late or a fact short. There was no relationship or proportionality between the remedy and the "wrong." None of our core values were expressed in such a jurisprudence. It was a search for perfection without regard to consequence. We were exalting formalism at the expense of substance and safety. It was wrong.

To my surprise, my colleagues in the audience responded enthusiastically to these remarks. A number of them later approached me and told how frustrated they feel by the meaningless obstacles that are strewn in their path. These are judges who take their jobs seriously. Unfortunately, the system gets in the way.

There are no simple solutions to the disorder of our courts. But I believe that our courts would work better if we made the following ten basic changes:

1. The vast and unknowable search-and-seizure laws, based loosely on the Fourth Amendment, must be simplified and clarified to prevent a guessing game on the street and in the courtroom. As long as the law remains unknowable, there is no justification for the mandatory exclusionary rule.

2. The *Miranda* ruling is an unnecessary overreaction to past abuses that videotapes and other technology can now preclude, and it should be abandoned.

3. Speedy trial statutes, based on a precise formula of days and weeks, only protect those who are most interested in getting away with crimes and manipulating the system. Reasonableness, not a ticking clock, should determine speed.

4. The right to an attorney should not be a factor in the investigative stage, but only in the pretrial and trial stages. Asking questions and receiving answers from a suspect is a legitimate aspect of crime-solving.

5. If it appears from the evidence that the defendant could reasonably be expected to explain or deny evidence presented against him, the jury should be instructed that they may consider his failure to do so as tending to indicate the truth of such evidence.

6. If defendants seek pretrial discovery from the state, they should be asked to place a written version of their story in a sealed envelope before receiving that discovery to preclude manipulation and lying.

7. Peremptory challenges should be limited to three or fewer to avoid stacked juries.

8. Unanimous jury verdicts are less likely to speak the truth than majority verdicts, and should be replaced by ten-to-two or eleven-to-one verdicts in criminal trials.

9. American judges should be allowed a more active role in the courtroom to assure that the process is swift, sure, and according to the laws of evidence.

10. The fact that, in recent years, an ever-increasing number of major criminal cases have had decisions reversed on technical (and often irrational) grounds, unrelated to our core values, demands we reevaluate our fundamental philosophy and procedures.

Finally, we should return to the premise that the criminal justice system is engaged in a search for the truth. For without truth, what can be the point of lofty principles? Without truth, how can our society properly maintain the ideals, values, and principles upon which it was founded? If, as Disraeli said, justice is truth in action, it's time for us to act.

ABOUT THE AUTHOR

HAROLD J. ROTHWAX has been a trial judge in the
New York State Supreme Court for over twenty-
five years, prior to which he was a defense attorney and card-carrying member of the ACLU.